"*78 Reasons Why Your Book May Never Be Published and —
Reasons Why It Just Might* belongs on every unpublished
writer's bookshelf—right next to *The Elements of Style*.
Reading it is like sitting down to a private meeting with
an industry insider. It's both a reality check and a pep
talk. Pat Walsh tells writers exactly what they need to
know."

> —Wendy Sheanin, events manager,
> A Clean Well-Lighted Place for Books, San Francisco

"In this business, we too often encounter people who want
to be authors but who don't do the work. These are folks
who dress the part, never revise, and are singularly inti-
mate with all eight forms of the verb *to be*. Pat Walsh's advice to those folks isn't pretty. But this little book could
be just the thing for writers who are willing to face the
odds honestly and to take the art, craft, and business of
authorship seriously."

> —Frederick Ramey, Unbridled Books

PENGUIN BOOKS

78 REASONS WHY YOUR BOOK MAY NEVER BE PUBLISHED AND 14 REASONS WHY IT JUST MIGHT

Pat Walsh is the founding editor of MacAdam/Cage, an independent publisher of fiction and nonfiction. A former reporter for the *San Francisco Chronicle,* Pat lives in the city with his wife and son.

78 REASONS WHY YOUR BOOK MAY NEVER BE PUBLISHED

and

14 REASONS WHY IT JUST MIGHT

PAT WALSH

PENGUIN BOOKS

PENGUIN BOOKS

Published by the Penguin Group

Penguin Group (USA) Inc., 375 Hudson Street, New York, New York 10014, U.S.A.

Penguin Group (Canada), 10 Alcorn Avenue, Toronto, Ontario, Canada M4V 3B2 (a division of Pearson Penguin Canada Inc.)

Penguin Books Ltd, 80 Strand, London WC2R 0RL, England

Penguin Ireland, 25 St Stephen's Green, Dublin 2, Ireland (a division of Penguin Books Ltd)

Penguin Group (Australia), 250 Camberwell Road, Camberwell, Victoria 3124, Australia (a division of Pearson Australia Group Pty Ltd)

Penguin Books India Pvt Ltd, 11 Community Centre, Panchsheel Park, New Delhi— 110 017, India

Penguin Group (NZ), cnr Airborne and Rosedale Roads, Albany, Auckland 1310, New Zealand (a division of Pearson New Zealand Ltd)

Penguin Books (South Africa) (Pty) Ltd, 24 Sturdee Avenue, Rosebank, Johannesburg 2196, South Africa

Penguin Books Ltd, Registered Offices:
80 Strand, London WC2R 0RL, England

First published in Penguin Books 2005

10   9   8   7   6   5   4   3

Copyright © Pat Walsh, 2005
All rights reserved

LIBRARY OF CONGRESS CATALOGING-IN-PUBLICATION DATA
Walsh, Pat, 1968–
    78 reasons why your book may never be published and 14 reasons why it just might / Pat Walsh
        p. cm.
    ISBN 0-14-303565-7
    1. Authorship—Marketing.   I. Title: Seventy-eight reasons why your book may never be published and 14 reasons why it just might.   II. Title.
PN161.W26 2005
070.5'2—dc22   2004060165

Printed in the United States of America

For my beautiful wife, Jeannine, who thinks I'm a wonderful writer despite all evidence to the contrary, and for my son, Jack, whose love of books rivals my own

"Always remember that if editors were so damned smart, they would know how to dress."
    —Dave Barry

ACKNOWLEDGMENTS

I HAVE THE BEST agent in the world in Amy Rennert and this book never would have come about without her hounding me to turn an offhanded idea into a manuscript.

The superb people at Penguin took my bitter ramblings and translated them into English and wisely asked me to cut a lot of exposition, many grammatical mistakes, and dozens of bad jokes. Jane von Mehren, Brett Kelly, and Jessica Rothenberg are the best triptych in publishing.

MacAdam/Cage publisher David Poindexter, my boss and friend, was encouraging and kind, as was the entire staff consisting of Avril Sande, Dorothy Carico Smith, the Jeffs, Anika Streitfeld, Kate Nitze, J. P. Moriarty, Scott Allen, Melanie Mitchell, and Tasha Kepler (who sent me moose jerky). Julie Burton and Jason Wood went above and beyond. J. A. Gray and Emily McManus handled first reads deftly.

I wish I could list all the authors it's been my pleasure to work closely with . . . oh wait, I can. They are: Dave Falconieri, Ken Goldberg, Ann Pearlman, Mike Patterson, Miriam Darvas, Joe Di Prisco, Alison Clement, Mark Dunn, Steve Elliott, Ed Cline, Diane Freund, Katie Towler, Noël Alumit, Elisabeth Hyde, Frank Turner Hollon, Bev Marshall, John F. McDonald, Norm Gautreau, Germaine Shames, Sonny Brewer, Craig Clevenger, Michelle Richmond, Joey Goebel, Amy Koppelman, Michael B. Oren, Ellen Potter, Michael Kun, Suzanne Hudson, Bruce Ducker, Stephen Inwood, Stephen Barnett, Alan Spence, Jonathan

Odell, Joe Formichella, Brian Francis, Will Christopher Baer, Ronald Everett Capps, Peter Temple, Dayne Sherman, Samantha Hunt, Sheila McGrath, and Jack Pendarvis.

Thanks to my family, whose list of names is almost as long as the one above, but here goes: Thanks Brendan, Maura, Brigid, Kathleen, Olivia, Dorothea, Fiona, and Vinny. Another special thanks to my parents, Vince and Dorothy.

And yet another enormous thanks to my wife, Jeannine, and my son, Jack, who put up with a lot of my crankiness and whining while writing this book.

If I forgot anyone's name, it does not necessarily mean I don't like you, but it just might.

CONTENTS

Introduction   *xix*

PART ONE: TALK IS CHEAP   *1*

1. The Number One Reason Your Book Will
   Never Be Published Is Because You Have Not
   Written It   *3*

PART TWO: A COLD, HARD LOOK   *11*

2. Your Book Is Not Good Enough   *15*
3. You Do Not Revise Your Book or You Will Not
   Revise It Again   *17*
4. You Think Too Highly of Yourself   *20*
5. You Think You Are a Natural   *22*
6. You Think Writing Is Easy   *23*
7. You Listen to False Praise   *24*
8. You Do Not Know What You Are Talking About   *25*
9. You Do Not Care About Language   *28*
10. You Cannot Tell a Story   *28*
11. You Preach   *29*

12. You Do Not Realize That Nobody Cares   *32*

13. You Are a Copycat   *36*

14. You Do Not Have Style   *36*

15. You Have Too Much Style   *38*

16. You Do Not Kill Your Little Darlings   *39*

17. You Use Bad Metaphors and Similes   *40*

18. You Sacrifice Clarity for "Art"   *41*

19. You Do Not Know Grammar   *43*

20. You Do Not Care About Syntax   *45*

21. You Do Not Know Enough Vocabulary   *46*

22. You Read Your Writing Aloud Too Much   *47*

23. You Have a Tin Ear for Dialogue   *49*

24. You Do Not Know Your Audience   *51*

25. You Do Not Trust Your Audience   *52*

PART THREE: THE PUBLISHING GAME   *55*

26. You Do Not Understand How Publishing Works   *57*

27. You Do Not Understand the Bestseller   *58*

28. You Do Not Understand the Selling of Books   *62*

29. You Do Not Understand That Publishing Is Not a
Game of Words, It Is a Game of Numbers   *64*

30. You Do Not Understand the Game of
Managed Risk   *66*

31. You Do Not Understand the Soft Science of the Profit-and-Loss Statement   67

32. You Do Not Understand Comparable Titles   69

33. You Do Not Understand the Agent Connection   70

34. You Do Not Understand Advances   72

35. You Do Not Understand the Auction   74

36. You Do Not Understand the Author's Role in Publishing   76

37. You Do Not Understand Publicity, Promotion, and Marketing   77

PART FOUR: THE OTHER PUBLISHING GAME   81

38. You Fell for Self-Publishing Hype   83

39. You Think Self-Publishing Will Get You Taken More Seriously   87

40. You Signed with a Pay-to-Play Agent   89

41. You Go to Writers' Conferences for the Wrong Reasons   94

42. You Found the Wrong Book Doctor or Editing Service   96

43. You Listened to Some Bad Advice   98

PART FIVE: SLUSH DIVING 101

44. You Will Rot in the Slush Pile as the Publishing House's Lowest Priority 103

45. You Are Kidding Yourself If You Think You Are Not in the Slush Pile 106

46. There Is Too Much Slush 106

47. You Are in Bad Company 108

48. You Are an Uninvited Guest at the Publishing Party 111

49. The Slush Pile, like the Publishing Industry, Does Not Make Sense 112

50. Enthusiasm Does Not Come from the Slush 113

51. You Missed Your First-Chance Glance 116

52. You Got Cute and Made a Fool of Yourself 121

53. You Made Stupid Mistakes 123

54. You Got Lazy or Impatient 124

PART SIX: AGENTS PROVOCATEURS 129

55. You Accidentally Went into the Junk-Mail Business 133

56. You Do Not Know What You Are Looking For 134

57. You Did Not Research Agents 135

58. You Did Not Go to Published Authors 136

59. You Submitted Your Work Too Early 138

60. Your Query Is Queer 138

61. You Cannot Stop Talking About Yourself   139

62. You Cannot Describe Your Own Work   140

63. You Lied   141

64. You Do Not Understand the Agent/Author Relationship   141

65. You Sullied Your Name   142

66. You Scare Away Agents   143

67. The Dark Side of Agents   144

68. The Agent Rejection   145

PART SEVEN: ACQUIRING MINDS   147

69. You Don't Know What Editors Do   149

70. You Do Not Know What Most Writers Do Not Know   151

PART EIGHT: BAD MOJO   153

71. You Have Bad Luck and Bad Timing   155

72. You Accept Bad Luck and Bad Timing   156

73. You Are Caught in a Topical Storm   157

74. You Blame the Publishing Industry for Your Lack of Success   158

75. You Do Not Take Advantage of Opportunity   161

76. You Are Sticking to Your Guns   162

77. You Do Not Go on to the Next Book   163

78. You Do Not Take Positive Action   164

PART NINE: THE GOOD NEWS   167

1. You Wrote a Good Book   169

2. You Are Honest with Yourself   171

3. You Do Your Homework   172

4. You Make Yourself Stand Out   174

5. You Have High Hopes and Reasonable
Expectations   175

6. You Have a Healthy Perspective   176

7. You Take Advantage of Time   177

8. You Are Patient but Persistent   180

9. You Are Flexible   183

10. You Learn from Rejection   184

11. You Take Calculated Risks   186

12. You Take Yourself Seriously   189

13. You Make Your Own Luck   190

14. You Have Fun   191

INTRODUCTION

MANY YEARS AGO, I tried to write a novel and failed. I failed miserably. I had a publisher, ample funding, time, a private office, a computer, and the support and faith of many. Six months after I began, my hard drive held tens of thousands of words that did not add up to anything; multiple drafts started and stalled. I had no book and no excuses.

It was the best thing that ever happened to my career as an editor.

I now know, reading manuscripts every day, what writers are trying to do, and where they are trying to go. I recognize the traps they fall into and the shortcuts they take. Most important, I now have a profound respect for anyone who sets out to write a novel and finishes it. Just because there are a lot of manuscripts out there doesn't mean that any of them were easy to write.

There is an old adage that says, "Those who can't do, teach." In my case, "Those who can't write, edit." That being said, the irony of publishing my first book about publishing a book after failing to write or publish my first novel is not lost on me.

I love editing and I feel I am good at it. I am not always right, despite what I may occasionally tell our authors, but I care about the books I edit and I want them to meet the authors' and my own expectations in terms of literary value, critical approval, and commercial success—in that order.

Being an editor is a strange job, unequal parts nitpicker

and structural engineer, advocate and taskmaster, artist and businessperson. It is a calling rife with rejection and criticism—both given and received—and glorious highs and devastating lows. My emotional and professional fortunes rise and fall with "my" books. Bad reviews fill me with rage and dread. Good reviews swell my pride, and I invent new ways to mention them in conversations with people I barely know. Peaks and valleys can be found on any given day. When I come home and my wife asks about my day, I start with the good news and end with the bad. There are always both to some degree and I love that.

The real trick to being a good editor is finding the right book. Most editors go about this by building relationships with agents to get included on early rounds of submissions so they can jump on the hot title. I do that, too, but I really enjoy the treasure-hunting approach to finding manuscripts because it suits my personality. To my wife's horror, at social gatherings I'll mention that I'd like to spend my retirement wandering a beach armed with a metal detector or going to flea markets. I watch *Antiques Roadshow* to see if any of my junk is worth millions. As a child, I lived for the arrival of *Highlights* magazine so I could play the hidden-picture game. Now I have the perfect job. To me, finding those few exceptional manuscripts among the thousands of also-rans is a thrill. It can also be an expensive, time-consuming, and mind-numbing task.

I do not know everything about publishing. I can only guess what makes an instant bestseller or what book will get people talking. There is no guaranteed way I know of to win critical acclaim and prestigious prizes. Like everyone in publishing, I have no incontrovertible knowledge, only be- liefs based on observation, experience, and gut instinct.

The defining characteristic of publishing, particularly fiction, is subjectivity. What is pure gold to one reader can be utter rubbish to another. Books inspire passion with readers everywhere but no more so than in my industry. (I have found, in publishing, that conversations about books we love frequently become spirited discussions about books we hate.) One of the worst moments editors face is finding a manuscript they love and then having all their coworkers and bosses hate it. There has never been a book published that every single reader has loved.

Because publishing is a business, great efforts are made to economically and mathematically quantify the very human aspects of the subjective in order to minimize risk. Opinion, passion, and emotion are realized on paper in the forms of multiple reading reports, profit-and-loss statements, and comparables—all to reach a comfortable level of confidence and perhaps, on rare occasions, consensus.

Three types of companies comprise the publishing world: Big New York, the academic press, and the independent house. I work at an "independent press," or, some might say, a small press. (All small houses are independents, but not all independents are small.) I have a great job. MacAdam/Cage was founded by David Poindexter in 1998 to publish writers, especially first-time novelists, whom the big, greedy New York houses, with their tepid taste and fear of risk, were ignoring for the wrong reasons. (We later learned that the big houses were not anywhere near as bad as we thought, and their commitment to literature was genuine, but it was fun to demonize them at the time.) David is my hero, despite the fact that I have often thought about throttling him. (I have asked around and this is not an unusual fantasy in the editor/publisher relationship.) Along with operations guru Avril

Sande, we learned the business from the ground up. Somewhere in the office sits a much-dog-eared copy of *How to Self-Publish Your Book,* from which we learned about ISBN numbers, copyright protocol, and the rudiments of distribution. The odds were, and are, against us but we lived in ignorant bliss. I am very glad there was no one around with publishing experience to tell us that it could not be done. We simply hung out a shingle, manuscripts started appearing, and we started reading them. We found, amid the many odd submissions, several wonderful books. Even after agents started submitting, we continued to till the mail bins looking for the gem that had been missed. It is a practice we continue to this day.

Several years and a thousand mistakes later, I am offering this book to make your job as a writer and my job as an editor easier. It is my attempt to help talented, dedicated writers become authors and bad, overambitious writers to become other things, like plumbers. We need more good plumbers.

Glibness aside, I hope this book accurately describes the current publishing situation and gives you, the aspiring writer, an honest depiction of this industry, warts and all. I also hope that, by pointing out mistakes you might be making, you will produce better material and submit it smartly and successfully.

Focusing on seventy-eight mistakes writers make is, admittedly, a bit cynical, because I am a bit cynical. I am under no illusion that finding your way to print is easy, and I have no interest in telling writers there are surefire steps or secret tricks to finding a publisher or an agent. If you are convinced there is a shortcut, then there are plenty of books on the market for you. Many of these books will tell you the secret is in the pitch letter—hook 'em right in, they say, grab the editor with dazzling marketing lingo, and so forth. This is simply a bunch of crap. Editors see hooks like old bass do, and we do not trust marketing plans from amateurs. What attracts us to queries and pitch letters is subject matter, an engaging tone of voice, and good writing. That said, there are many valuable books on publishing. I refer to them throughout this book.

I do not believe presenting the publishing situation sunny-side up is doing writers a service. I will not tell you there are three easy steps to getting an agent, simple tricks to get editors to pay attention to your book, or secret handshakes that will get your book published. I will tell you that the competition you face is stiff, the odds against you formidable, and the journey ahead arduous. I will tell you that after reading this book you should be better prepared to avoid mistakes and act productively. This is all any book on publishing can ever honestly give you.

After telling you the seventy-eight things you might be doing wrong, the last part of this book, "The Good News," offers hope for those who are serious about their writing and willing to learn from their mistakes. The writer who focuses on fundamentals—primarily developing the quality of the writing—will triumph over the writer who spends all his time researching catchy cover-letter copy, sending out bushels of unripened manuscripts, and reading up on zany marketing ideas.

The publishing industry, for all its flaws, respects the serious writer, regardless of genre. We seek authors dedicated to their work, professional in manner, and with optimistic but reasonable expectations. These are not easy people to find, mainly because everyone thinks they are one of those people. This is not true.

Most people who write a book have ambition, which differs from dedication. With ambition, the goal is the key element. With dedication, the process is the prize. The committed writer values the creation of the book; the hungry writer values the publication of the book. That is not to say that dedicated writers do not care if their books are published; they do, but it is not the only reason they write them.

If all writers toiled at their desks fine-tuning their prose, refrained from sending out first drafts, or called it quits after reading their own works and pronouncing them unfit for print, the publishing world would be a different place. Promising large advances, houses would advertise for authors. The daily mail call would be a time of anticipation instead of dread. Agents would not exist.

This is not the reality. Many writers send out drafts as fast as their printers can spew them forth—sometimes without even spell checking. There are those who have been told for years that their writing is wanting but who still believe they are misunderstood geniuses. And agents do exist. Good thing, too, we need them. These days, agents are publishers' first line of defense.

From an editor's perspective, the most important role an agent plays is that of filter, separating not just good manuscripts from bad, but professional writers from people with a typewriter and too much time on their hands. Now, with agents more overwhelmed by submissions than editors, writers seeking to become authors face an increasingly difficult task: acting as their own filter, separating their wheat from others' chaff. (Adlai Stevenson once described editors as people who separate the wheat from the chaff and publish the chaff. Smart-ass.)

Great writing is unnatural. It is not simply a gift. It is not genetic. The power to use words—to tell a story, to make people understand what they do not know, to make them see what they could not imagine before—is a talent, and talent is not given or taken. Talent is earned, through dedication, hunger, and care. It is born of a desire to share the fruits of imagination and experience with readers, just as you have been educated and entertained by the labors of other writers. It grows from a commitment to making others see and appreciate what you have seen and appreciated. Thoughtful writing is a way of replenishing the well from which sustenance has been drawn.

People who write for the wrong reasons, who do not read, who are motivated only by personal glory and public fame are not what I consider writers. They are narcissistic typists and they are the reason many good writers will never have the chance to find their place on the bookstore shelf.

I am writing this book to give writers a true account of what publishing is like, because you cannot beat the odds if you do not know them. The picture looks gloomy and perhaps a bit maddening; but as one of my favorite quotes, a Chinese saying, goes, "There is great disorder under heaven and on Earth and the situation is excellent."

Before all else, writers must be honest, and not just on the page. They must face their abilities and failings. There is a great temptation to blame the publishing industry for their lot. If getting published is truly your goal, you must resist this temptation, accept the industry's failings, and adjust.

The book business has always been a tough business but never as tough as it is here and now. Americans do not buy a lot of books compared to other countries such as Germany and Spain. When they do, they tend to buy the same author over and over—particularly novelists. Recent surveys have shown that the readership for books is down, and that trend does not look likely to abate anytime soon. This does not leave a lot of room for writers to break in and it certainly makes earning a living as a writer a near-impossibility.

Only a small percentage of people who write a novel will ever see it published. I would guess one half of 1 percent. Of those authors, a much smaller percentage will earn enough from their books to be able to write full-time. My guess, again, is one half of 1 percent. Of that lucky group, I would, once again, guess that only one half of 1 percent will reach the pinnacle—bestsellerdom, with its attendant money and fame. The point can also be made thus: I have been told more people win million-dollar jackpots playing the lottery every year than get their first novels published.

Why is it so hard?

Because it is supposed to be. Being a novelist is the best job in the world, so it is—rightfully—the hardest job to get. It should not be easy to get published. Imagine, for a moment, that it was. Everyone who had a typewriter and some spare time would have a book in print. We would live in a world of literary garbage. People who love to read would have to sift through hundreds of bad books to find a passable one and hundreds of passable books to find a great one.

Actually, that sounds a lot like my job.

78 REASONS WHY YOUR BOOK MAY NEVER BE PUBLISHED

and

14 REASONS WHY IT JUST MIGHT

PART ONE

TALK IS CHEAP

You have made some notes, read some writing books, and done some research. Mostly what you've done is talk about writing a book. An idea for a book is not a book; it is a waste of time. There is no singular thing that makes someone a writer, but there is one thing that makes someone a joke— talking about writing a book without doing any work.

1. The Number One Reason Your Book Will Never Be Published Is Because You Have Not Written It

You might read that last sentence and silently add the words *not yet* to the end. I think *yet* is the worst word in the English language. Besides being the weakest way to begin a sentence, *yet* is the biggest excuse at a writer's disposal and therefore one of the most overused. If I ask an aspiring writer, "Have you finished your book?" and he answers, "Not yet," I can usually, and safely, forget his name.

Life is full of Not Yets. I sometimes think people feel that meaning-to-do-something is related to actually-doing-something. They are distant cousins at best.

What we mean when we say "Not yet" is "No." *Yet* implies that something is imminent, and the writing of a book is never imminent. It takes a very long time and is not finished until there is nothing you can think of to make it any better. If you are not at that point and someone asks if you have written a book, answer honestly: "No. I just started," "No. I'm still working on it," or "No. I've written a couple of drafts but it's a ways off still."

Honesty is every writer's goal, even in fiction, and treating your work truthfully will help you and others take it seriously. Exaggerating your accomplishments will only cheapen you and add the unwanted pressure of having to do a lot of work just to get to the point you have told people you are already at.

Worse, you might begin to believe the lie, and then you are doomed. If you have told your friends and family you are writing a book, they may keep asking about it, even if you have made no progress. So you fill them in on a plot breakthrough or a new character you have created. Soon, instead of talking about what you have done, you find yourself talking about what you intend to do. Maybe you have talked about your "book" so much, you feel it's actually finished in your head and all you have left to do is type it out. A simple chore you have not made time for. Yet.

Ask yourself these questions: Before one whole chapter is finished, do you have a cover in mind? Have you already come up with a sequel? Have you settled on the perfect cast for the movie? Have you taken an author photo? Have you spent more time telling people about the book you're writing than you have actually writing it?

If the answer to any of these questions is yes, then you are not a writer—just a talker. You may even be coming very close to being a blowhard. An idea for a book is not a book, no matter how good the idea is (and many are not very good, unfortunately). A synopsis, an outline, a pile of notes is not a book. Most important, the act of writing the book is never perfunctory, no matter how much you have fleshed it out in your head or mentioned it at cocktail parties.

I cannot count the number of times I have expressed interest in a book pitched to me only to find out that it is not written yet, "but will be very soon." Send it to me when it is done, I will say, and they will promise me a manuscript in the not-too-far-off future and I will never hear from them again. One talker who promised to send in a manuscript three months hence finally did—three years later. The book was sloppy and rushed, so I passed.

On the other hand, suppose you have studied your craft, written a manuscript, done the tedious revisions, and been brave enough to send your baby out into the world of rejection and apathy. Now, when someone asks if you have written a book, you can smile and honestly say, "Yes, I have." Please enjoy the moment of pride because, in a second, that person is going to say, "Has it been published?" and your face is going to fall. Take heart: Since a publishing contract could be imminent, you are now free to say, "Not yet."

If you have not written at least a completed, revised draft, then the following pages will be of little use to you. You can return this book to the bookstore and get your money back or use it to prop up a table leg. It also makes a fine beverage coaster for two drinks. This book, and most others on the subject of publishing, will be helpful only to those who have already written a book. Books on writing can help you avoid mistakes, improve your technique, and even provide motivation and inspiration, but books about publishing require a manuscript as a platform to be of any real assistance. If you are thumbing through this book in the bookstore seeking a guide to hone your writing skills before venturing on to writing a full manuscript, put this book back, save your money, and glide left down the shelf to *The Elements of Style* by Strunk & White.

Now and then at a writers' conference or some such gabfest, I will be asked what makes a "real writer." Being lazy by nature and eager to please, I will spout off a few meaningless concepts like dedication, perseverance, love of writing, blah, blah, blah. It seems to satisfy most people. They nod their heads and smile as if I am describing them to a T. I don't really understand this question. "Real writer?" The only price of admission to the club of writers is the act of writing. As far as I am concerned, any hack who writes limericks can call herself a poet; any fool who sends his fantasies in to *Penthouse* Forum can call himself a magazine journalist. Who cares?

The purpose of the question "What makes a Real Writer?" is to validate a fictitious hierarchy among writers; to separate those who are active in the community—attending conferences, reading *Granta,* and, for some reason, wearing beads—from those who sit alone at the typewriter banging out a political thriller, a detective novel, or a sentimental memoir not dealing with a crazy mother, suicide, or incest.

Many writers consider themselves "real" to differentiate themselves from the novice and the workman. And I think it is a dangerous waste of time. If you want to elevate yourself above others as a writer, then do it on the page. Every second you spend worrying about your rank in the swells of the unpublished or slightly published is a waste of time.

It is a cliché to say writers write because they are compelled to, but it is true. What is not always true is that writers write because they are compelled solely by a love of the literary arts. Ambition, fear, hubris, and revenge are often motivations for—or at least contributing factors to—an author's drive. The forces that create writers are similar to those that create politicians. Of course, elected officials want to serve the public and make the country safer and more prosperous, but they also want to see their face on a poster, bask in the public's adoration, feel respect, wield power, and prove something to their families and friends. Writers, I have found, have to write, even during the often-long periods when they do not produce much. The old saw is that writers have to write because they are useless at everything else. As for the definition of a "real writer," I know only this: When I look at the authors I have worked with and the authors I know, there is little common ground among them. The only shared element I sense from all of them is a particular balance of ego and insecurity.

Ego is what makes a writer start writing, believing that, even in a world of Shakespeare, Hemingway, Clancy, and Cartland, there are not enough stories. Through the lens of ego, a writer can clearly see that the world of books is lacking and needs his singular contribution. Ego is a potent force but it needs to be tempered.

Insecurity is what drives creative people to better their art. Insecurity is the engine of dedication, making one study, learn, reflect, anguish, and, of course, revise, revise, and revise.

When one of these two forces is overly dominant, or even missing, the result is disaster. By itself, ego is the ancestral land of bad writing, where a hack thinks her quickly jotted prose, by its very nature, is the best thing ever written. This woman sends it out into the world and confidently waits for the parade of publishers to march up her street bearing million-dollar advance checks. When this does not happen, which is every single time, she feels like an unrecognized genius.

When insecurity is the sole occupant of a writer's psyche, either the book is never written because the first sentence is never deemed good enough to move on to the second or it is never sent out for fear of the inevitable rejection and ridicule.

In the rare instances when the forces of ego and insecurity are juxtaposed just so, a mental vortex forms and the conditions for strong writing and an original voice are born. I can imagine such a writer reading a book and saying to themselves, *I can do better than this.* I can also imagine this same writer reading his own work and admitting sheepishly, *I can do better than this.* Perhaps, *I can do better than this* is the "real writer's" credo.

If you have not written a book but are seriously considering doing so, there are some things you need to know. The first is that there are tens of thousands of books written every year by first-timers and only a small percentage of them will be published. I would not be surprised if the millionth word a writer has written is the first one published in a book. As for the big paycheck you hope to get, I would venture that when the amount earned, even by a well-known author, is divided by the number of hours spent reading, studying, thinking, writing, and revising, it is less than the minimum wage. Given the amount of time it takes to write a good book, working at McDonald's makes more financial sense. In a nutshell: Getting published requires an unholy amount of work and a great deal of time. It is often closer to the culmination of a career rather than the beginning of one. If you are looking for a hobby and enjoy writing, then by all means, have at it, but know that being published is a long shot in the best of circumstances.

After reading all this, some may ask, "Aren't you afraid you might have dissuaded someone from writing the great American novel?" No. I do not believe anyone with the drive and talent it takes to be an author will be dissuaded by hearing what he or she has probably already figured out.

Recently, I met with a young woman who reminded me how many roads to nowhere there are between writing and publishing. The woman—whom I will call Lindsey, because that is her name—was referred by a coworker from MacAdam/Cage's sister corporation who had gone to high school with a friend of her father and she wanted an informational sit-down. (The sheer fact that Lindsey felt the need to throw such a wide net to find a publishing connection startled me a bit.) I agreed to meet with her, as I have with everyone interested in publishing who has ever bothered to ask me.

We sat down and she handed me a résumé. I quickly ascertained that she hoped the informational interview might turn into a job interview. She had recently graduated from college and had met with some other publishers and agents regarding employment opportunities. I started to blather on about editing, complained about agents, and dropped a bunch of names . . . the usual. When I paused long enough to ask her what aspect of publishing she was interested in pursuing, she flatly told me that what she really wanted to do was write novels and short-story collections. Why then, I asked, was she trying to break into an industry that she clearly did not want to work in? As my preposition dangled in the air, she gave me a suspicious look: *Was I testing her? Or was I an idiot?* She assumed I knew that getting published is about whom you knew—a closed system available only to the inner circle. Working in publishing was a way to pay the bills while getting into the game.

I asked her what she was doing to pay the bills now and she told me she was a bartender at a colorful local pub. That is the perfect job for a writer, I told her. You are not stuck in a cubicle, filing reports and ordering toner cartridges. You are surrounded by the human element at its best and worst and every place in between. Most important, you can write before work when you have time and energy instead of after when you are tired and the couch and television seductively beckon. You have the perfect situation for a writer, I told her. She was unimpressed.

"You need the connections to have your work taken seriously," she told me.

"Well," I said, "I will take your work seriously. Do you have a book?"

Her response: "Not yet."

PART TWO

A COLD, HARD LOOK

Your pride and joy, your baby, the fruit of your labor is most likely not well written, at least not enough to see the publishing light of day—it may even stink. There are plenty of other reasons your book may never be published, but all of them combined do not equal this reason: Your book is not good enough.

FEEDBACK IN PUBLISHING is most often mealy-mouthed and euphemistic. When we hate a book we say, "I didn't fall in love with it as much as I had hoped to." When we think the story is lacking we say, "I didn't connect with the story the way I need to." When we say something is too small, too quirky, too special, we mean it will not sell. When we think the writing is bad we say it is too commercial or too plot-driven.

Editors and agents do not give blunt advice and criticism very often. It does not do any good, because the writer almost always reacts defensively and stops listening. Criticizing someone's writing in a candid way is an awkward endeavor. Nobody wants to hear it, even those who consider themselves thick-skinned. So, instead, we wilt and temper our strong opinions down to polite, suggestive remarks that may even be mistaken for praise. A writer's first response to criticism is almost always defensiveness, which does not lead to anything constructive and makes the editor feel like a heartless jerk. When confronted with direct, blunt criticism, there is a natural reaction, especially when dealing in creative matters, to respond with denial. But cold-hearted analysis is what is most often needed—if, for nothing else, to ensure that the message is not diluted. It is not easy to look someone in the eye, talk to them on the phone, or even write them a letter flatly and dispassionately telling them they have failed in their efforts. I am as prone to fold in the face of confrontation as anyone in the industry. Although, I must admit, it is a bit therapeutic being a cold-hearted sommabitch, albeit a cowardly one, here late at night in my kitchen writing this.

2. Your Book Is Not Good Enough

The main reason your book, after you have written it, will not be published is because it is not good enough—it probably even stinks.

When I say your book probably stinks, I mean statistically, it probably stinks. Of the roughly four thousand submissions our publishing house receives a year—unsolicited and unagented—at least half reek of bad writing and sorry story lines. Another thousand significantly lack in one area or the other. The next eight hundred are not horrid, just not good enough—mediocre efforts, rife with clichés and tired plots. Of the two hundred left, I would say a hundred and fifty have some real merit but are a good idea badly executed or a bad idea nicely realized. From the fifty remaining, forty are heartbreakers—almost but not quite there. In some way, that is difficult to explain other than to say it usually manifests itself when a reader puts down the manuscript and is not excited about picking it back up. Or they fall apart at a crucial stage in a way that is difficult or impossible to fix. The remaining ten are very good and a few of them are exceptional.

This crap-to-gem ratio is the reason why most publishing houses do not read the slush pile seriously and why agents depend on referrals to find clients. Writers know this. The problem is, they all think they are the wheat and not the chaff. That is true for a precious few; if you are going to be serious, then you have to go on the assumption that, while your book, as it stands, has some merit and a lot of potential, it probably needs more work.

In this book, I am addressing writers who are approaching the adult trade, a term that sounds a lot sexier (or sexist) than it is. The adult trade is fiction for a general audience, usually older than thirteen, and nonfiction titles that are not explicitly technical or academic in nature and are available in normal retail channels. The areas I am focusing on include literary fiction, commercial fiction, romance novels, mysteries, thrillers, anthologies, short-story collections, memoirs, autobiographies, biographies, narrative nonfiction (fact based, but reading like a story: think *Into Thin Air*), political exposés, and so on. I cannot really focus on children's books, computer manuals, prayer books, coffee table books, poetry, and how-to books because I do not know enough about those branches of publishing to be the flippant know-it-all I aspire to be.

So, why do so many manuscripts stink? There is no shortage of reasons, but the most obvious is that not enough writers are honest with themselves about their own work when they have the chance to be. Determining the level at which parts of your book stink is your job as a writer. Just because your book stinks, it is not a waste. Writing is a process and writing crap is an important part of any author's career.

Every few years, an announcement will be made that a "lost" manuscript of an important writer has been found in a desk drawer or steamer trunk. The writer's estate will raffle it off to the highest bidder for a quick buck. I guess what we are supposed to believe is that the author wrote the book and misplaced it or forgot about it and would be happy to have the manuscript published. I think there was a very good reason she stuffed it into the back of a drawer or locked it away in a trunk. The writer did not want it published because it was not very good. Even great writers write bad books.

You have to be tough on yourself. Here are three true statements to get you started: Just because you wrote something does not mean it is special. Just because you meant the words does not make them meaningful. Just because you like your characters does not mean anyone else will. You may feel discouraged by this news, but who cares. You are the only one who can decide how good your book will be. If you don't give a damn, then no one else will.

3. You Do Not Revise Your Book or You Will Not Revise It Again

All publishing clichés are true (except for "Publish or Perish," which is a bit hyperbolic). The truest is this: Writing is rewriting. Rewriting is the surest way to take both yourself as a writer and your book seriously. One of the best things about being a successful writer is being the master of your own fate, and nothing epitomizes this more than a revision when you have the luxury of taking as much time as you need to make your manuscript perfect. Take advantage of it now, because once you are published, agents and editors are going to be pressing you to finish the next book.

The best source for revision is yourself if you can be honest and distance yourself from your own work. If not, you need to develop those skills or find someone who can be blunt—and who also knows what they are talking about regarding language and storytelling.

There is a tic in the mind-set of most writers that gives them a sense of double vision regarding their own work. They conceive an idea, flesh it out somewhat, and write it down—just as they are supposed to. Instead of letting the work rest for a while—a week, a month, a year—they print it out and decide it is ready to go straight to press. A few are even unaware of the concept of drafts.

Reading the manuscript after completing a first draft and changing some character names or small plot details is not a revision; neither is moving a sentence or two around or retitling chapters. There are many things that a revision is not, but it is hard to define what it is. The common elements of a solid revision are letting some time pass between readings so missteps stand out, and looking critically for redundancies, weak language, exposition, and continuity issues.

My favorite baseball player, Will Clark, hit a home run on the first pitch during his first at-bat in the major leagues and he did it off Nolan Ryan in his prime. Sure, anything is possible, but are you willing to bet your career on being the Will Clark of writing?

Too many writers, warped by the thrill of typing "The End," think they have hit a home run on the first pitch. I really believe that 90 percent of the manuscripts submitted to editors and agents are first drafts and this is a terrible thing. Several years ago, a man called me to say he was sending in his wife's book. She felt it was premature, but he was an educated man, an avid reader, and he knew a great book when he saw one. She was just being humble. His enthusiasm was so strong it breached my protective shell of skeptical apathy and I read the book as soon as it arrived. The wife, of course, was right. The manuscript showed some promise but was thick with rookie mistakes like dead-end plot branches and flowery exposition. I made a list of what I thought were gently phrased suggestions and called him back. I did not get to pass on my thoughts after my delicate rejection because the husband hogged the conversation with a detailed explanation of where I could put my head—a place even years of yoga training would not help me reach. It turns out he had sent the book in with such confidence that he expected to present his wife with a publishing contract as a surprise for her upcoming birthday. I do not know if he was just that proud or just that cheap.

Odder are the scribes who are under the impression that it is an agent's or editor's job to guide them through every rewrite or even do it for them.

Some writers refuse to revise until they have a book contract or an agent. To them, I offer the sage advice of philosopher St. Thomas Aquinas, or was it Pee-Wee Herman: See ya! Wouldn't wanna be ya! You want people to invest money and resources in you when you will not invest a sliver of time in yourself? It is like saying you are not going to put on a suit for a job interview, but you might if you get the job.

4. You Think Too Highly of Yourself

Writer's hubris is a key ingredient in bad prose. When inflated self-worth is an overwhelming force, the results can be stub-your-toe, chew-on-tinfoil painful.

I have met several writers over the years who are very intelligent, so much so that they are hamstrung by intellect. They are not trying to write the best they can at the moment, they are trying to upend the literary world and publish a magnum opus right off the bat. Ambition is good, but it is clear these writers are simply trying to show everyone up—like someone who decides to enter politics by running for governor of California. It is great to aim high, but writers like this are not even trying to pen the best-written book ever; they are trying to write the most important book ever—one that will bring a torrent of controversy, glory, and, eventually, immortality. Most of the time they end up with only sour feelings and a bad book. *My book isn't bad,* they say, *you are just too stupid to understand its Joycean/Pynchonian/Proustian subtextual wordscape.*

Yep, that's right. It would be easy to be an author if the only person who had to understand your writing was you. What this writer is really saying is that he is nothing short of a genius, a literary lion, unfairly unrecognized in his time. To him I say, put this book down, Einstein, and trawl from coffeehouse to coffeehouse with your 985-page manuscript under your arm while you wait for Philip Roth to return your letters. Just don't send the thing to me; I do not have time to read inaccessible, badly executed, ill-conceived pap by a writer who knows it all. You may think your book is the next addition to the canon of literature, pure and unsullied by the dirty paws of correct grammar and spelling, but it is overwhelmingly likely that it is important and precious only to you. My advice for these writers is to go read paragons of simplicity such as *The Old Man and the Sea* and *Animal Farm*.

By happenstance and, um, luck, I once came face-to-face with a writer whose book I had rejected. He asked why and I, fortunately, remembered the novel enough to comment that I was confused by strange references that kept popping up. Those, he told me, were inside jokes about Samuel Johnson. I pointed out to the writer that Mr. Johnson has been dead for two hundred years and had nothing to do with the manuscript's story. No one, I told him, was going to understand these references. He smiled wryly and said, "Not yet. But one day . . ." He was assuming the day would come when there would be a field of study devoted to the deconstruction and debate of his work à la James Joyce. I wanted to tell him, "You do not get to completely redefine literature or change the world to your own ideal with your first book. If Joyce had started with *Finnegans Wake,* he would have had a one-book career—if that. You will not break into the canon and make critics and professors rush to study every nuance of your work and your life. Your first book will not spawn imitators. University libraries will not bid for your papers. Has it happened before? Yes, a few times in the last hundred years. Are you counting on that?"

I wanted to tell him all this, but my pizza was getting cold and he had more deliveries to make.

Let me be clear. If you are determined to shake the core of literature and write an instant Pulitzer Prize–winning classic, do not let me stop you. I would hate to be the reason *Moby-Dick* or *Angle of Repose* was never written. You want to shoot for the stars and be published? Then be like NASA and get a plan, deliberate and bold, and execute it with precision and care.

---

5. You Think You Are a Natural

Many writers feel that they are instinctive artists who can craft moving stories, bold dialogue, and structured, clean paragraphs on the first draft. These writers have no use for training, no time for revision, and no chance of seeing the light of day.

In my time in publishing, I have met only one true natural, someone who learned writing from reading other novels but does not emulate or copy. His first drafts are clean, his stories varied and original, and his dialogue honest and sharp. He can, and has, written great books in very short amounts of time, seemingly from his fingertips straight into print. He is Frank Turner Hollon, and despite his uncanny skill, he is open to editing suggestions and revisions and never considers himself above criticism. He is always looking for ways to improve his craft by experimenting and reading. If you are like Frank, congratulations, go forth and prosper. If something tells you that you are not, get to work. Writing is tough going; God help you if you think otherwise.

6. You Think Writing Is Easy

As a rule of thumb, if you are having an easy time writing something, something is amiss. Sure, you will have streaks and go on a nice run now and again; but as a whole, it is not easy. The only time writing is easy is when you are drunk. But the next day, you will wonder who broke into your house and wrote that horrible drivel.

Most writers have learned from the frustrating experience of staring at an uncooperative blank page. But a few others have not. They won an award for the best five-paragraph essay in eighth grade or won a short-story contest in college and have felt writing is a cinch ever since. They feel past praise is an excuse for discontinuing their betterment as writers. They forget that you can get good grades in a writing class without having talent, as long as you exert effort and have good organizational tools. They forget, too, that grades do not count after you graduate (Personal note: Thank God!). Great writers do not rest on their laurels and they do not ever feel they have produced their best work. They look for areas in which they have failed so they can improve and they want feedback that is honest and blunt. They know that biting criticism may hurt, but misguided praise can harm.

7. You Listen to False Praise

Your spouse, your children, your friends, and your family are usually bad judges of your writing, even if they hold degrees in literature, are very tough critics of books in general, or are published authors themselves. Listening to friends and family gush about your storytelling and writing skills is good for your vanity, but do not believe it. Enjoy it if you want to, but don't believe it. Do not believe them when they tell you they think your book is wonderful. What they mean is that you are wonderful or the fact that you wrote a book is wonderful. The only people's opinions that can help you are those who do not care about you at all.

People who love you have not paid twenty-five dollars for the privilege of reading you and they probably have nothing to gain by hurting your feelings. Or they could just be really gullible or have bad taste. Or they might have liked your book or even loved it, but there's probably a really good reason they're not in publishing. Sometimes people who know you will overlook problems with your writing and they will inflate your abilities. They will doubt their own instincts and opinions and sometimes they will just lie. You should appreciate their praise, magnify the significance of their criticisms, and seek objective, knowledgeable opinions.

By the way, your worst fears are probably true. When, after gushing about your book, someone close to you mentions a couple of tiny things they did not understand, it is a huge problem you did not see. When they waffle about the writing, saying they are unqualified to judge or too stupid to understand your literary talent, they hated it. If they did not know you, and read your book, they would boldly announce that the author was an idiot or the book was garbage.

Only you can be the judge of who is a good reader for your material, but I think most serious writers look for venues other than family and friends to help appraise their work to ensure objectivity. Writers' groups can be invaluable tools in vetting material and they have the added benefit of allowing you to hone your own critiquing skills. Writers groups continue where M.F.A. programs end. They allow writers to gather and either be supportive of each other or beat each other to a pulp.

8. You Do Not Know What You Are Talking About

You should not write a book about something you know nothing about. Does that seem obvious? Judging from many manuscripts, it is not. Many people think that a little imagination and a lot of artistic license supersedes knowledge and research. It does not. The old adage, like so many old adages, is sound: Write what you know. If you do not want to, then at least do the necessary research—meaning more than you could possibly use in the actual book—so you don't look like a fool.

Ask yourself, how much research have you done? Are you really conversant in your topics? Did you know the area first, or did you come up with a plot or character background and then try to meld in a few details from an encyclopedia or magazine article? It is important to realize that a reader can smell when you do not know fully what you are talking about even if they do not know anything either.

When a writer chooses to expound on subjects they know nothing about, it is a constant source of amusement for me. People who have interesting backgrounds, unusual jobs, or colorful personal histories often choose to ignore the obvious and find a writing subject far removed from their own fields and personal experiences. Bartenders writing potboilers about human cloning, morticians writing exposés on economics. I once received a query from a tugboat captain—his book was about a farmer. Is the grass always greener? The exception is lawyers, who almost always write about lawyers, usually idealized versions of themselves fighting for justice and getting lucky.

I understand that familiarity breeds contempt. It is hard to see your own situation as anything other than old hat, but readers might not agree; and your credibility will rise if you have a background in your subject. Charles Bukowski wrote *Post Office* about his decades of services in one of the most boring jobs in the world and it is one of the funniest and captivating novels ever written.

Obviously, if you are writing about Mars in the year 2184, or England in the sixteenth century, or your characters are fish, then you cannot tap the well of direct experience, but there are things about your life that will be valuable to your book. How your characters see themselves and their world, what their motivations are, how they interact with their situation are all universal points in fiction. If a writer does her job right, then how she sees the world will come through no matter what the plot or setting. Almost every book is to some degree a comment on the human condition; so what you feel and think has bearing, even if your characters are not human.

If you have chosen the path of creating a fictional or alternate reality as the setting for a story, then you must remain true to that world and that is not easy. I suspect that some writers feel that if they create their own world in which to set a story, they can just make everything up and not have to worry about research or continuity mistakes. I disagree and think the best works in the various genres bear me out. J. R. R. Tolkein, Isaac Asimov, and Philip K. Dick created stories in alternate realities in such a way as to leave the reader feeling it was real. I am only guessing, as I am too lazy to do my own research, but I would bet they created their worlds separately from their stories and did not fake it as they went along.

As a practical matter, when writing about the distant past or far-off future, there is a temptation with new writers to either idealize or demonize characters—the belief being that we used to be more pure of heart and/or will eventually become so. Unless carefully considered, this habit can lead to stereotypical characters and predictable plots.

In fiction and nonfiction, knowledge of your writing subjects, from geographical settings to character details to minutiae, gives your imagination a basis for telling a story. Be careless and your ability to engage the reader will be damaged.

9. You Do Not Care About Language

It is hard to imagine someone who does not care about language writing a book, but it happens a lot. I do not know whether these people have too much time on their hands or if they need to prove something. They think that writing is a rote exercise and only the marketing, personal connections, or other business factors are how books get selected. They are like conspiracy buffs and cannot be dissuaded from their beliefs. They think what they are writing completely overshadows how they write it.

If you do not think writing is important, even in plot-driven genre novels and practical nonfiction, then no one can help you. You should find another channel through which to deliver your thoughts. Writing is the medium with which you have chosen to express your ideas; you had better love it or you are going to waste a lot of your time (and maybe some of mine).

10. You Cannot Tell a Story

I know a golfer who plays three times a week and has for more than ten years. He reads books, watches videos, and goes to the driving range but his game never gets better. He does not play golf because he likes to, he plays golf because he cannot accept that he cannot play golf.

A good storyteller takes his responsibility seriously, making sure the way he relates his narrative is respectful of a reader's time and intelligence. Readers need a reason to turn a page. They want to be invested in what happens next or hunger to know more of what the author is talking about.

The ability to tell a story can be likened to the ability to sing. Singing can be trained, it can be honed, it can be refined, but it cannot be taught where there is no foundation. Similarly, many people do not have the learned or instinctual ability to tell a story. They cannot grasp the entirety of a narrative or see a thorough line of character development in relation to plot circumstance. They cannot see that their story does not make any sense. They spend pages describing useless details and gloss over important points and critical scenes.

Thankfully, the vast majority of people who have no storytelling talent do not become writers. When someone lacking storytelling abilities embarks on a career as a writer, she is doomed and that is sad. She will fail with all her might.

---

11. You Preach

Writers are passionate and passion is a powerful thing. Like most powerful things, it often cannot be trusted in the hands of the people wielding it. The most common abuse of passion is the tendency—nay, the overwhelming temptation!—to give in to preaching.

Preaching stinks up the page like ripe fish and makes the editor's and agent's job of rejecting a book quick and easy. Unlike most writing problems, it cannot be fixed because the book is almost always built around the problem. The book doesn't make a point; the point is made into a book.

In nonfiction, preaching is straightforward and easy to dismiss: prose composed entirely of someone telling the reader what is right and what is wrong. The audience for this writing is the usually tiny sliver of the population that agrees 100 percent with the author; the book is just an excuse to bang the table and say "damn right."

In fiction, things are slightly subtler but far more annoying. All told, preaching is perhaps the most common flaw I see in manuscripts. The following would not be far off from what is submitted every day:

Caitlin Greencloud has returned to her tribal reservation in Northern California's Headwater Forest after receiving her Ph.D. in Ecology Studies at Yale only to discover that the last old-growth redwood stand on the Pacific Rim is at risk from loggers and developers bent on clearing the trees and building a golf course and country club, and oil refinery. But Caitlin has discovered a Forestry Service Environmental Impact Report that would prove that road construction and runoff mitigation will negatively impact the Marsupian squirrel population, already on the endangered species watch list. But Assemblyman Bill Buckingham, under the thumb of the logging and construction industry, will stop at nothing—including murder—to quash the E.I.R. until the California Coastal Commission vote is cast and only an unlikely appeal to the Republican-controlled E.P.A. will save the squirrels . . .

Or, on the flip side:

> *Former Major General Ivan Staskakovich has been waiting*
> *thirty years for this day—ever since the Berlin Wall came down.*
> *America had been too strong, he thought, for too long. Now, after*
> *years of a Democratic Congress and two terms of a liberal*
> *President, the time was ripe. Ivan knew his time was coming*
> *when President Lillyliver let gays join the military even while*
> *cutting defense spending, allowed immigration to run unchecked,*
> *and declared guns illegal and sent troops door-to-door to confiscate*
> *them. Building a new Soviet army in Cuba was easy since*
> *Guantanamo Bay Military Base was closed. As Ivan poured*
> *over a map of Nebraska trying to decide on the perfect spot for his*
> *winter Dacha, he mused to himself, Didn't those fools learn any*
> *lessons from the movie* Red Dawn? *Thousands of miles away,*
> *one man, another soldier, was thinking the same thing. Sgt. Jake*
> *Jackson knows of Ivan's plan and has a plan of his own . . .*

Yes, I can write that badly. For whatever reason, the novel is the favorite medium of both environmentalists and Constitutional enthusiasts—or tree huggers and gun nuts, depending on your politics.

I have seen all forms of preachiness—cultural, political, moral—and all of them are ugly, particularly the viewpoints I agree with. If I read a text that endorses a philosophy or opinion I share, and the writer is preaching at me, it makes me feel I have aligned myself with the wrong side. How, I ask myself, can I be in the same camp with this bore?

If you are inspired by an opinion or viewpoint, then by all means incorporate it into your writing. But do not make it the entire reason for the book's existence and do not blatantly tell readers what is right and what is wrong. Show your readers an honest situation, warts and all, and let them decide. Let them exercise their own judgment and come to conclusions if they want to; but let us enjoy the story and writing on its merits.

Even in religious organizations full of the already converted, leaders try to tailor their messages to be dynamic and meaningful because they know they cannot simply say something is so and have people take it to heart. Even Jesus, Mohammed, and Buddha did not preach much; they all used devices like parables and aphorisms to let the follower draw the lessons. People can barely take it when they think it is coming from a priest, a prophet, or even a god; why would they take it from you?

---

12. You Do Not Realize That Nobody Cares

Not much is sadder than an entire manuscript, whether it be novel, memoir, or narrative nonfiction, about a subject no one cares about. There are plenty of them out there being sent around, generating a blizzard of rejection slips. Everyone who picks up a book hopes it will be special and writers are trying to fulfill that hope. Somewhere along the line, however, many writers lose the ability to discern between what is interesting to a reader and what is interesting to them.

I once read a woman's novel about the circumstances around her firing from a local industrial firm. There was no plot other than the minor conspiracy involving her supervisor and a coworker whom she claimed had sabotaged her computer and time cards. There were long descriptions of mundane job duties. The only color was frequent references to the coworker's fake breasts and the boss's bad breath. I lightly suggested to the author that she did not need a publisher; she needed a shop steward. But she was convinced that the novel would be her ultimate vindication and the masses, or at least her coworkers, would take to the streets demanding justice.

Write what you know may be a truism, but it is not a license to bore the pants off everybody. If you are a structural engineer and want to set your novel at a structural-engineering firm, then go ahead. Use your inside knowledge to add authenticity and intricacy, but do not cut yourself a slice of life that makes other people want to end theirs. Use imagination, plot, irony, imagery, humor, depth, nuance to make it interesting. Otherwise, ask yourself honestly if your subject would be better served as nonfiction if it really needs to be in book form. Maybe it would make a better magazine article in a specialized journal.

When something is very important to you, it may be hard to see that it is very unimportant to most everybody else. If you feel a personal catharsis when writing or reading your story, this might be a bad sign. It can be therapeutic to write about a personal situation that has no larger context, but please recognize that it is not publishable if for no other reason than to spare yourself the inevitable disappointment.

Narrative nonfiction writers and novelists who use themselves as the basis for their protagonists must beware of falling into the deep pit of narcissism. Readers are not going to care about you simply because you care about you. They read between the lines and can smell when writers base characters on themselves, even if you call yourself Jake Savage or Belladonna Belize. They form impressions based on how you treat yourself. If you describe yourself as having a devilish smile or Michelle Pfeiffer-esque grace, they are going to know it is you. It is kind of like being caught posing in front of the mirror. Incidentally, calling yourself Jake Savage or Belladonna Belize does not help either. If the character is based on you, then do what you do, hopefully, in real life. Do not toot your own horn, be as honest as you can, and be a little self-deprecating.

Sadder than the author who has wasted a lot of time or embarrassed himself is the author with a great story that has simply been told too many times to generate enough sales and attention to justify publication.

After the success of *The Greatest Generation/Band of Brothers* franchises, a great swell of World War II memoirs and personal histories began circulating. Many were bought and published to great fanfare, but eventually sales waned and interest faded because the public's tastes are fickle and its attentions are flighty. While a few subjects are stalwarts—namely, the Civil War and losing weight—most come in and go out of favor over years and decades.

The saddest victims of publishing's cyclical whimsy are those who write the dire and tragic memoir, stories of cancer and the Holocaust. Terrible as it is to say, a Holocaust survivor's cleanly written memoir recounting brushes with death and memories of loved ones probably will not be published today unless it has a hook we have not heard before. Cancer is another topic that publishers are overwhelmed with. It is kind of sick and I feel bad about it, but if an editor tries to sign up a book about surviving the Holocaust or cancer, there had better be a new take on the story or the higher-ups are going to roll their eyes: *Not another one*. The sad truth is that the genre is currently considered overpopulated.

Talking with an agent once, I mentioned that I'd just found a memoir written by a cancer survivor that I was interested in acquiring. "Oh no," she said with a tsk-tsk shake of the head. "Cancer's dead. But India's hot." I felt so very proud of my chosen profession at that moment.

I have been waiting a long time to say this: If you took a road trip in college with your best friend, a lover, or a diverse group of buddies, keep it to yourself. The road-trip novel is a slush pile lifer—a constant source of sophomoric writing and forced humor involving bodily fluids and disdainful authority figures. It is the most tired, most beaten-to-death premise in entertainment since Hollywood decided it would be funny if adults were trapped in kids' bodies and vice versa.

Hunter S. Thompson, Jack Kerouac, and Homer perfected the genre. I am going to go out on a limb and guess you are not in their company. If you insist your story is too funny, crazy, and poignant to leave unwritten, then go write a screenplay.

Most of the Nobody Cares books are copycats anyway. After *Tuesdays with Morrie* was a success, a spate of imitations featuring young mixed-up yuppies finding wisdom from the older generation poured in. While publishing certainly is not shy about trying to repeat success, we know unrelated knock-offs are money losers, not to mention professionally embarrassing.

13. You Are a Copycat

Some aspiring writers read a novel and notice the author's cadence; some read a work of narrative nonfiction and notice strong argument construction; some read a magazine article and take note of a clever turn of phrase; some read a short story and notice a subtle but powerful metaphor. Most writers learn from these things; but some retype them into their computers and change the proper nouns.

Learn from reading, by all means, but do not copy. Just because someone is having success writing a certain way with certain characters in a certain style does not mean you should "borrow" their shtick. All writing has influences but copiers reach well beyond homage toward blatant stealing. I see this a lot in the thriller and mystery genres.

Besides being ethically wrong, it never works artistically or commercially, at least not in the long run. It is much better to develop your own style. You will know you have succeeded when other people start copying from you.

14. You Do Not Have Style

If you were so inclined, I guess you could analyze in great detail a few writers' work and quantify their style into a pattern of sentence structure, vocabulary, syntax, and so forth. People do this, but I do not get the point. All they learn is that each writer's style is a reflection of the writer's perspective and imagination in relationship to his use of language. Duh. That said, I have my very own, overly simplified theory on writing sentences.

As a sentence part, the noun is the easiest to work with. I cannot think of an instance where I told a writer, no matter how bad, that he failed in his use of nouns. If you have problems with nouns, you are really in trouble. The verb is a bit trickier. Colorful, specific verbs make any writing better, but the perfect verb is sometimes hard to find and the "to be" variant is always seductively nearby. Carefully placed and sparse adjectives can make good writing spicier but they can also distract. Besides, the adjective is the part you want the reader's imagination to fill in from the context. Adverbs and prepositions are the level where great writers play. The elements get smaller as the skills get higher. As in many endeavors—sports, cooking, art—the seemingly minute is where the greats distinguish themselves. When a real pro has to use four prepositional phrases in a row, it is because it does not work any other way. Readers do not even notice, because they are engrossed, invested in the material, and the writing is fluid.

A good writer makes you forget that you are reading. Bad and lazy writers constantly remind you that you're looking at words on a page.

Fearing mistakes or charges of purple prose, many write in a string of simple declarative sentences sprinkled liberally with pronouns and forms of "to be." The simple declarative sentence is one of the most powerful tools in a writer's box; but if it is overused, it loses its impact and makes writing boring. The same goes for long sentences filled with loosely constructed prose and repetitive words and phrases. It doesn't have to be grammatically incorrect to be bad.

15. You Have Too Much Style

The writer who has too much style is the person who cannot say something clearly. She uses every trick in the book, breaks every rule, and even makes up a few of her own words to ensure she is unique. She usually succeeds—to the worst possible end. Her writing is a crazy quilt no one can enjoy unless they are on acid. Her writing is a load of incomplete or overly complex sentences, pompous words, and punctuation-free sentences à la Molly Bloom.

The verb tense is the favorite playground of the style forcer. Every week, a manuscript arrives at my office in which the author believes he is the first person to think of writing present-day scenes in the past tense and flashbacks in the present.

A writer who tries to force style into his work overuses devices for the sake of device. Needless ornaments—such as unjustified multiple points of view, not italicizing characters' thoughts, removing paragraph breaks so everything runs together—risk distracting from the book and hint that there is very little meat on the bone.

Fred Astaire once said that if you make enough of the same mistakes long enough, people will consider it your style. That may be true in dancing, but not in writing. Style is born of a writer's love of language, not her ignorance or laziness. When a deliberate writer's style deviates from the boundaries of grammatical rule, it is to expand language's power and influence, not flout it. So if you want to elevate sloppiness to art, become a tap dancer, twinkle-toes.

16. You Do Not Kill Your Little Darlings

A little darling is a piece of writing, sometimes as short as a single word and sometimes as long as a whole scene, that the writer thinks is brilliant, profound, pithy, or jarring—but no one else does. It is the thing he fights to keep in no matter how many people tell him to take it out. To the writer, a darling is evidence of his brilliance, and everyone else be damned.

Darlings are particular to every writer, so finding your darlings is tough. One way to discover their troublesome presence is to get feedback from a reader you can really trust, but the best way is to find them yourself by rereading your manuscript with a very critical eye. Your darlings will pop out at you and you must, no matter how painful it may be, strike them.

Killing darlings is no fun and is one task that makes writing a chore, but it has to be done. Every author has to do it at some point. I see darlings in every first draft of every book I edit. I draw a line through them, indicating they should be cut, and invariably the revision comes in with the little darling intact. I am not surprised anymore because I know little darlings are survivors, like cockroaches. They last from one revision to another because the writer has fallen in love with them and will not let them die. Even as they cut scenes, plot threads, and characters, the darlings remain.

Darlings usually fall into two categories: clever and precious. Clever usually shows up in dialogue, where a character says something colorful or snappy out of place with her motivations or the plot circumstance. Precious pops up in description, usually in metaphors, where the writing hits an abrupt note and the reader is left wondering why.

The first sentence of a manuscript is the primary nesting place of darlings because the opening is the genesis of the whole book. Changing it would be a betrayal to the whole impetus for the project. Get over it. A book is a living, breathing thing until it goes to the printer. Nothing is immune from scrutiny. As for what to replace it with if it has to go? I believe the first sentence of your book should be the best sentence in the first chapter. You build from there.

---

17. You Use Bad Metaphors and Similes

Metaphors and similes exist to add clarity and emphasis to make the complex and nuanced more familiar and informative to a reader. Metaphors and similes are devices and, like all devices, they have a purpose—they are not meant to be purely decorative. If they are used correctly, not only is the point made, the device adds color and mood. As emulators of Raymond Chandler know, it is not easy to come up with "It was a blonde. A blonde to make a bishop kick a hole in a stained glass window." Experiment with colorful comparative devices but temper everything with scrutiny so nothing ridiculous gets through.

Everyone believes they write good dialogue and metaphors. If only wishing made it so. Far too many writers slip into clichéd or tortured exposition when they invoke the metaphor. What can I say: Metaphors are a bitch and similes are tough as nails. Too many writers rely on metaphors, making description do the work of the action, or verb.

The exception to the rule may be Southern authors whose styles are steeped in a tradition of ornamentation and literary gingerbread. Where great writing is an intricate mosaic of vibrant vocabulary and atmosphere is built on dialectical color. Where a simple declarative sentence is considered an insult.

Lucidity is the basis for comparatives. I once read a pretty good manuscript, but the author's use, or misuse, of similes kept tripping me up. He wrote about a mountain man walking over a hillside and hearing the sound of "the wind blowing through the tall conifers like a chorus of murmurs from the depths of the ocean." Pretty phrase, if that is your thing, but it does not make any sense and it does not serve any purpose. I am no Daniel Boone, but I do not need any help understanding what wind blowing through treetops sounds like. If the character was on a rowboat in the Atlantic and heard a chorus of murmurs from the depths of the ocean, I would not know what that sounded like. His conifer simile might help me stay in the book and not get confused.

18. You Sacrifice Clarity for "Art"

I appreciate beautiful writing for its own sake, but when you are telling a story, relaying information, or making an argument, it is a disservice to your reader if you stop being clear so you can add a bit of poetry to show how pretty you can write. This sin is often committed when the subject or narrative demands a simple style but the author is afraid to use it in the event readers think her incapable of high art. Or, I suspect, some writers throw in gobbledygook to make something simple seem complex and deep. Then there is the writer who peppers his prose with anachronistic phrases and fifty-cent words to make himself feel superior. To them I say, stop being so sesquipedalian or consider self-defenestration.

All the words on a page should be there for a reason, and that reason must be evident to the reader. If they are not, use the delete key liberally. This does not mean your work should be dumbed down or without nuance. Write complex sentences and use the perfect word if you can find it, even if it is obscure—just take care that what you are saying is not getting lost in how you have chosen to say it. Readers like being treated intelligently and they like learning new vocabulary from context, but they do not like to feel lost. If someone reads your book and keeps getting confused, they will not blame themselves for not being smart enough, they will blame you for not being good enough. I have talked to writers who have written parts of their book in a deliberately muddled way in hopes of making the critics pay more attention. I wish they would focus on another medium, like performance art, where there is no standard, no rules, and no me.

19. You Do Not Know Grammar

Writers who are serious, even if only to themselves, give a damn about how they are saying what they are saying. They know and care about the rules governing the English language, even if it is only with an intuitive sense. Writers are hungry to learn what they do not know, especially about their craft.

I am not going to attempt to summarize all grammatical laws here, but if you do not know the basics, go learn them. There is no shortage of texts on the subject and you should read several. Many of the books are entertaining, such as *Eats, Shoots and Leaves, Woe Is I, Good Grammar Made Easy, Bryson's Dictionary of Troublesome Words,* and, of course, *The Elements of Style* (read the entry for *flammable/inflammable* in the chapter on misused word and phrases). You should familiarize yourself with the *New York Times* or the Associated Press style books. The truly ambitious should attack *The Chicago Manual of Style* (and if anyone ever figures out how to use its index, please, let me know).

How familiar you are with grammar before attempting to write a book is up to you, but I think you should know the parts of speech, verb tenses and modifiers, sentence and paragraph construction, and the difference between active and passive voice. The most productive way to learn is to diagram a few of your own sentences. If you feel sentence diagramming is a remedial chore best suited for kids, you are right. So are multiplication charts, table manners, and toilet training. If you have not learned those by now, you should. Do not give prospective publishers another reason not to take you seriously. Also, you should memorize how to conjugate *lay* and *lie* so you can act superior around other writers and advertising copywriters.

Some people complain that strict adherence to grammar is a moot exercise. Even if that were true, people would still care about bad writing, wooden and flat or purple and long-winded. Those things are born of inattention to grammar and syntax. It is not fun to read and no one will buy it or give it prizes.

As for punctuation, it is not difficult to acquire a solid, working knowledge in a relatively short time. For some strange reason, punctuation intimidates many people, even those who want to be authors. Give punctuation a day—just one day. Get a grammar book, start at page one, and cross out everything you already know. Spend the remainder of the day reviewing what you are unsure of. Periods are easy. If you are having trouble with periods, you should take another look at the whole wanting-to-be-a-writer thing. Commas can be tricky, but not prohibitively so. Colons are straightforward. Semicolons are usually misused or overused and should be avoided. But, for the love of Pete, learn how to use an apostrophe. It is not hard and it is screwed up so often it is discouraging. (God, I hope I didnt misuse any or I'm going to get some snide letter's.)

20. You Do Not Care About Syntax

Syntax is not, as I once assumed, the reason my regular breakfast—three cigarettes and a couple of shots of root beer schnapps—costs too much. Simply put, syntax is the order a writer chooses to put his words in. Easy, no? Then music is just a bunch of notes in a certain order and art is just splotches and strokes on a canvas. Most writers have a grasp of grammatical rules, decent vocabularies, and something they want to say. Where they fail, or rather fall short, most often, is by failing to massage their syntax from correct to effective.

The writer must be mindful of how she is saying what she is saying. Each sentence has an emphasis and intended purpose. It does not matter if it is you writing a book about cats or James Joyce writing *Ulysses:*

> *Mr Bloom nodded gravely, looking in the quick blood-shot eyes. Secret eyes, secret searching eyes . . .*

This could have been written another way, with the same words, even fewer of them, and come out like:

> *Mr Bloom nodded gravely while looking in the quick, blood-shot, secretive, and searching eyes.*

Or worse:

> *The secret searching, blood-shot, secret, and quick eyes were looked into by a nodding Mr Bloom gravely.*

Revising a manuscript is not just finding typos and plot omissions, it is a chance to shape your writing and build your voice. When you exercise and experiment with syntax, you will find your writing becoming more colorful and tonal with a defined cadence that will eventually be your style. Every sentence, paragraph, and chapter should be deliberate and every word should matter. If it does not, cut it.

The danger, of course, lies in the temptation to change something simple, hoping to achieve panache. Resist.

---

21. You Do Not Know Enough Vocabulary

I just read a submission with a lot going for it, but the author used the word *fetid*. It is a vivid word and it was used correctly each time, but he used it four times in the first six pages. Overusing a specific word not only implies that the writer is slothful and careless, it also lessens the impact. (I say this knowing I am guilty of the same thing in this book, but I already have a book contract.)

Clearly some words are excused from the rule—names, conjunctions, simple verbs. It is the specific, the strong, and the memorable you want to avoid overusing, usually verbs, adverbs, and adjectives.

Varying the word choice can be tiring, but it is worth it lest a reader assume you have a limited vocabulary or could not be bothered to grab a thesaurus. There are many thesauri on the market. Flip through a few at the bookstore and find one that is organized in the way you think.

22. You Read Your Writing Aloud Too Much

Do not read your work out loud to yourself as a form of revision. Unlike the other picayune gripes I have, this one is an indirect practice rather than a direct-to-page misstep. Why then is it listed here? Because when you have adopted the habit of reading your prose out loud, it shows in your work in a bad way. The inflection of voice hides a multitude of sins by emphasizing the colorful bits and glossing over the deficiencies. Specifically, writers who read their prose aloud tend to overstuff their sentences with prepositional phrases and needless words. Spoken ideas need more air to sink in; written words do not because the reader's mind goes at its own pace rather than the speaker's.

The exercise may be useful in the end stages of revision to ensure dialogue sounds authentic and the flow of the prose is even. It should not be used when writing early drafts.

Even books with a conversational tone suffer when recitation is used as editing, because the flow needed to sound "right" differs from the flow needed to read "right."

I admit I talk out loud to myself when I write, but usually only to ask larger questions like, How the hell did I talk myself into writing this book? Who's going to buy this book when it's in a store next to *How to Get a Million-Dollar Book Advance*? and I wonder what's on TV right now?

I have a little secret, which I have tried to hide from my authors. I hate readings. I go to them to show my respect and support and I love the idea of people coming together to celebrate literature. I do not generally enjoy readings because the way an author interprets his own work may not be the way I do, which makes me feel like I am reading something wrong. The idea of reading something wrong is absurd, of course, because good writing encourages the reader's imagination to participate in the story. Most authors love it when someone has a different (but still positive) interpretation of their work.

I know a writer I will call Mr. Wrongturns because he makes them all. Mr. Wrongturns has every ingredient to be a first-rate author—intelligence, drive, and time. Unfortunately, he also has every unwanted affectation, bad habit, and harmful misconception in the Will-Never-Be-Published Writer's Handbook. For reasons passing comprehension, I began speaking with him several years ago and we still talk on a regular basis. Our relationship is based on two things: my giving him the best advice I have to offer—and his doing the opposite. If I tell him to revise a manuscript, he abandons it and writes another. To date, he has submitted seven book-length novels to our house in five different genres. I do not really know why I keep taking his calls and reading his endless submissions, but I do. One of Mr. Wrongturns's favorite things to do is call me urgently to read me something he just wrote. I used to silently listen to him read while plotting my escape off the phone. Then I tried something different; I made him send new material. When he called, I read it to him—in a monotone. I left all feeling, emphasis, and cadence out. He was silent for a moment and then stammered, "But it doesn't sound good when you read it like that." I told him that is the way it reads on the page and unless he wanted to follow every person who bought his book home and read it to them himself, he had better get to work on improving his writing. It was the only time he ended one of our calls first.

The spoken word and the written word are cousins, not identical twins. Each has its place and needs to be respected, but a writer's focus should be on the page and he should not let a vocal bias mask his weaknesses.

---

23. You Have a Tin Ear for Dialogue

The hardest thing to write is a sex scene. The second is humor. The third is dialogue. Dialogue bedevils authors and most think it is the hardest thing to get right. Every writer I know approaches dialogue differently. One waits until her entire book is done and then adds dialogue. Another comes up with the dialogue and uses it to build his characters. Both methods work but it is never easy. Most writers eschew long dialogue scenes because they become distracting and do not generally convey a great deal of information or move a story forward. Dialogue works best when it reveals the relationship between two, or sometimes more, characters.

Great dialogue is so rare I wonder if it is a gift rather than a skill. Most writers can easily visualize their characters but few seem able to hear their voices. Poorly written dialogue tends to run together, leaving the reader wondering who is talking. Some writers mask this by adding contracted dialect or an accent or giving a particular character some idiomatic tic, like a hippie who begins every sentence with *dude* or a teenager who peppers his speech with *like* and *um*.

If you can read a line of dialogue with no context and still know who is speaking, the author has done a great job. Great dialogue is memorable and telling. It does not include expositional chitchat like:

> *"Hello," I said.*
> *"Hello," she said.*
> *"How are you?" I said.*
> *"Fine. How are you?" she said.*

Summation is a better tool in these instances, such as:

> *We exchanged banal pleasantries.*

Do not try to spice up your dialogue by adding too many synonyms for *said,* like *replied, explained, exclaimed, shouted, whispered, whimpered, pleaded,* or *yelled.* Also, do not stick a hokey modifier on *said* to add color:

> *"Hello," I said firmly.*
> *"Hello," she replied meekly.*
> *"How are you?" I inquired bravely.*
> *"Fine. How are you?" she answered languidly.*

24. You Do Not Know Your Audience

In one sense, you should not. Gertrude Stein got it right when she said she wrote for herself and strangers. Write to your best ability and when thinking about a reader, picture someone you have never met and never will. Never have your friends and family in mind or you will be hobbled by worries about what they think. Could you write a steamy sex scene if you worried about what your mother might think? Could you write completely uninhibited about a relationship that turns murderous, or infidelity or even marital dissatisfaction with your spouse in mind? It is difficult to maintain a high degree of honesty if you are concerned about misperceptions from loved ones.

But that is not really what I mean by not knowing your audience. Every book type has an audience with its own expectations. Your task is to know what those expectations are and exceed them. If you are writing a fiction genre book— thriller, mystery, noir—your audience expects engaging story lines, characters faced with dire situations and challenged by moral absolutes, and evocative settings. If you are writing a practical nonfiction title, your audience expects information delivered in a helpful manner and they do not want any questions in their minds at the end of the book. If your book is narrative nonfiction, your reader demands evidence of research through detail and accurate description. Lovers of literary fiction want finely tuned prose and some comment on the human condition. Readers of how-to books about publishing are sick of waiting and want the author to get to the damn point.

So here is the point. Do not write in a genre or form that you do not read or care about. I speak from experience. I abandoned the quirky book I wanted to write to start a potboiler because I thought it would be easy and fast. I was a moron. I did not read plot-driven commercial fiction. I thought it was junk so I thought writing it would be a snap. I wasted valuable months and ended up with something I would be ashamed to let anyone read.

---

25. You Do Not Trust Your Audience

If people who write books are so smart, why do they not know people who read books are smart, too? Maybe even—gasp!—equally so? So many writers assume their potential audience is incapable of imagining or visualizing anything not directly conveyed by the author. Sometimes authors even feel the need to repeat an important element several times. Is it an irrational fear that readers lack the ability to draw a conclusion? Or make a reasonable assumption?

When writers decide that readers are stupid, plots and narratives fall apart to become rote and boring.

The ideal contract between author and reader is based on mutual respect and admiration. You give me your time and money and not only will I not insult your intelligence, but I will engage it boldly. Act today and I will give your imagination a free massage, too.

When writing or rereading your manuscript, you must give the audience the benefit of the doubt. Trust them to be as sharp as you think you are. If you write something you would not need to be told or have explained to you, take it out. In an ideal world, every reader would be able to pick up a book and have absolutely no risk of being bored or insulted. In an ideal world everything a writer writes down is magic.

PART THREE

THE PUBLISHING GAME

You lack—or actively ignore—any knowledge of the industry you are trying to break into. While it can be counterproductive to focus too much on working in the industry, a rudimentary grasp of publishing is essential.

26. You Do Not Understand How Publishing Works

Burgeoning writers and those who care about books can hold idealized and romantic views of the publishing field. They imagine wood-paneled offices and oak desks, not a glimpse of Sheetrock or a cubicle in sight. A leather coach behind the thick-framed door from which novelists sleeping off hangovers startle their editors coming in to work. Stacks of manuscripts line the halls. Blue pencils and green visors lie about. The printing press is in the basement while the publisher's office, with a wet bar or silver tea service, is in the penthouse. There are three-piece suits, ink-stained fingers, Underwoods. There are spectacles, elbow patches, and tweed—miles and miles of tweed.

I think people in the industry perpetuate the myths about publishing for personal reasons. On the odd occasion when people seem impressed when I tell them what I do, I certainly never try to dissuade them. It is nice to have others think your job is mysterious, interesting, or sophisticated. And it is, just not in the way most people think. Then again, no cool-sounding job ever lives up to expectations. I once met someone who told me she worked for the circus. I asked, wide-eyed and eager, What is that like? There is a lot of paperwork, she said.

Needless to say, this idealized view is wrong and I don't want to waste a lot of time addressing publishing misconceptions. By the way, I am aware that I sound like I am aggrandizing my own industry and I know the vast majority of the populace couldn't give a damn about publishing's image one way or the other. I am just talking here about writers who do. Give a damn, that is.

At first glance, publishing is just another industry. We produce a product, bring it to the marketplace, and entice people to buy it. We study trends and try to quantify what makes a product successful so we can repeat it. We advertise, distribute, and promote. We have sales forces, production meetings, and conventions. We have business trips, business lunches, business cards. We have pie charts. We brand. When authors are not looking, we refer to books as "units."

Unlike other industries, our product is a book, arguably the highest form of human endeavor. The book is the conduit by which most of the greatest minds ever known have chosen to, or been compelled to, communicate with the world. Art historians may take issue; but in art, there is only one original, whereas a book has more impact as more copies are produced. Everyone I have met takes that guardianship seriously, though, admittedly, to various degrees.

27. You Do Not Understand the Bestseller

We all know the tales of books that come from seemingly nowhere to dominate the bestseller lists, making the authors overnight millionaires and guaranteeing them a full-time writing career for life. Every writer has a little dream or a big hope of making the *New York Times* number one spot. Judging from assurances I have read in cover letters, some writers have nothing less than a resolute expectation of selling more copies than the Bible. Writers seem well versed in which bestsellers are similar to their manuscript and how big their potential audience is.

What is not well known is the amount of time, work, and money—not to mention luck—that goes into the creation of a bestseller and how those decisions are made. I should mention that if I knew all the secrets of making bestsellers, it is doubtful I would be telling them for fourteen bucks. The way publishing works at the massive bestselling level—the ins and outs of Stephen King and Tom Clancy—are pretty much a mystery to me and most people in publishing. For a rare few authors who have become worldwide brand names, the publishing experience is vastly different from the one with which I am familiar. Big publishing clearly works because Danielle Steele's house is bigger than my high school and because, at her baby shower, every expectant mother in the country is issued a coffee-table book with pictures of newborns dressed up like bugs. Why every bestseller has a different trajectory to the top basically comes down to this: the right book at the right time with the right marketing. If anyone has completely figured out where to find the right book, precisely when to publish it, and how to market it perfectly to every potential reader in the country, they are keeping it to themselves.

Even the term *bestseller* can mean different things. Some industry people say as long as a book makes three bestseller lists in three cities, it can be called a "national bestseller." I learned this when one of our books made the local bestseller lists in three small cities in the Northwest, all of which were flukes. I could not, in good conscience, announce that it was a national bestseller. (Actually, conscience had nothing to do with it. I did not learn about this practice until too late.)

In standard terms, a legitimate national bestseller is a book that has appeared on one or more lists that gather data from nationwide sources including large independent bookstores, wholesalers, and chains. Those lists are compiled by *The New York Times, The Washington Post,* the *Los Angeles Times, USA Today,* and *Publishers Weekly.* Everything else is a local or regional bestseller, appearing on lists compiled by local bookstores that fax in weekly results to the local paper. Unlike smaller lists, the national lists have rules and formulas, considered proprietary, to safeguard against fraud and error. Good thing, too. A few years ago, an agent tried to buy an enormous number of his client's books from a store that reported to the national lists, not knowing that such large single orders are ignored. The store got a huge sale and the agent and author got a mouthful of embarrassing press. The book never made the list.

Generally, the first ingredient in big books is the announcement of a big advance, getting the bookseller's attention. Then a large printing of advance copies to give to bookstores and reviewers across the country follows. Book reps, salespeople who call on all the places where books are sold, are dispatched with orders to alert everyone that a book will be a surefire seller. They back this up with a marketing plan that includes a far-reaching author tour, national advertising, and a big review push. The promise to bookstores being, *You stock the book, we'll sell it for you.* Then the promotion department starts sending copies and press kits to newspapers, telling them this is the book everyone else is going to review, so they had better assign it now. Then they go after radio stations and television shows, letting them know that the author is hot and if they do not book him, someone else will. Pretty soon, the book has got tons of reviews and press bookings, it is sitting in the front window of all the bookstores, and readers cannot turn their heads without seeing the cover.

So what can go wrong? Everything. The entire process can fall apart at any level for a variety of reasons. The reviews can all be bad, the bookstores could decide to make small orders or not prominently display copies, media appearances can be canceled at a moment's notice. Another book with similar themes can be released earlier and steal the thunder. Usually, it is just a case of apathy. Bookstore owners, chain store buyers, and media bookers have heard it every week and they are not easily convinced. Sometimes everything can go right but the public will not respond.

The safest path toward a bestseller is if the author's last book was a bestseller. This is why the lists are dominated by very familiar names like Grisham, King, and Roberts.

So why do writers need to know about how a bestseller is made if they have no influence over the process? Because writers need to know that the book—on its merits—is the primary tool in breaching the lists.

Publishers will take risks on new authors because they can still be profitable even if they do not hit the top of the charts—and there is always the chance they could. Rarely, however, does a publisher take a debut book and give it the big investment, hoping it will shoot to the top.

Instead, they will take the first step and send galleys— paperback bound copies of the book, usually produced as early as possible—to booksellers and reps to read. If the book is very good, the better chance it has of generating interest. The book may strike a chord and a word-of-mouth movement will start. The publisher will respond and invest money in promoting the book earlier, which might propel it further along the road to wide success.

Word of mouth is the main engine of bookselling. Everything else we do—media efforts, review attention, and promotion—are all tools to get people talking about the book around the water cooler or in a Tuesday night book club. People trust their family and friends a lot more than they trust reviewers and certainly a lot more than they trust an advertisement. Advertising is just a way to remind people to buy something they've already decided to purchase.

28. You Do Not Understand the Selling of Books

I have been asked many times, or at least I will pretend to have been for the purposes of this chapter, what do publishers want? Easy. Depending on the who you are talking about, we just want to publish important books that change people's lives, inspire young minds, give people joy, or teach them something of great value. We want to help expand the body of literature, define a new genre, or perfect an old one. Give readers a thrill or a much-needed escape. We want to inform and teach. Effect change where it is needed. Make people laugh, cry, think. Build their own aquarium, cook a duck perfectly, feel warm and fuzzy about their cats.

Be a better boss or a happier person. Find a new job or inner peace. Change the world. Lose a few pounds. These sorts of things.

We cannot do any of those things if we do not sell books; and we can't do squat if we are not in business. Publishing houses differ in their philosophies, practices, and priorities (some even avoid asinine alliteration). But we all want to sell books—every single one of us, from Random House to the Communist Workers' Press.

All of this may seem blindingly obvious, but many people sit down and write books even they know will not sell but they still believe will be published. Their story is so important to them it simply must be published. I am always shocked when I read a cover letter that includes something like, *I know my book won't sell very many copies, but still . . .*

We do not offer book contracts based upon personal whims. We acquire books because we believe they will find an audience—not always an enormous one, but one that will cover the cost of publishing and at least make some profit.

We send our book reps into stores to convince booksellers our books will sell. If they fail to do so on a continuing basis, the bookstore will stop ordering our books, regardless of their literary or informational value. It is not a matter of greed as much as it is a matter of survival.

Some writers may scoff and say publishers are obsessed by bestsellers and do not give a damn about quality, but they are wrong. Do we want bestsellers? Yep, but for more than the filthy lucre. Big profits allow us, publishing houses and editors, to take more chances. If an editor with a recent bestseller under her belt finds an offbeat book that no one else seems to want, her bosses are going to be much more amenable to trusting her than if the editor has had a string of also-rans. The best editors in the business are some of the biggest risk takers—and vice versa.

The bad news for writers is that publishing is a complicated margin business that takes years of experience to truly appreciate. It is constantly changing, so your knowledge has a variable shelf life. The good news is, as a writer, you need only a fundamental understanding of the gristly innards of the commercial end of things. But you do need some.

---

29. You Do Not Understand That Publishing Is Not a Game of Words, It Is a Game of Numbers

Here is a breakdown of a book in the marketplace. Of the 100 percent of the retail hardcover sales price, say $24.00, an average 50 percent discount is given to the book wholesaler, distributor, or bookseller. The $12.00 left is divided as follows: Roughly 10 percent of the cover price is spent on the hard costs—paper, printing, film—of producing the book: $2.40. The author gets 12.5 percent on average over the first 15,000 copies shipped, or $3.00. The sales reps, those who entice booksellers to order the book, get 10 percent, or $2.40. Shipping books generally runs 3.5 percent, $.84. That leaves $3.36 per book to pay for all salaries, promotion, advertising, support materials, mailings, postage, shipping costs, rent, utilities, insurance, travel, and in my case, a personal manservant. A shipped copy is not a sold copy, even if the publisher has been paid for it, however. Once you convince bookstores to order your books and display them prominently (a privilege for which they often charge the publisher), the seller pays the publisher about half the cover price at some time in the future, ideally within a couple of months. If someone buys a book, the bookstore keeps the profit and everyone is happy. If no one buys the book within the first six months, the bookstore can send it back to the publisher or distributor for credit with which to order more books.

There are other income streams. If the publisher owns foreign rights, they can license them to overseas publishers in exchange for an advance and royalties, but the publisher does not always acquire these rights. Some publishers allow other, usually larger, houses to acquire the rights to publish paperback editions—which have a longer shelf life and lower production costs with a higher profit margin—in exchange for an advance. The money brought in is split with the author fifty-fifty.

There are also ways to lower expenses. Printing expenses go down as you print more copies. It costs half as much to print forty thousand books—on a per-book basis—as it does to print ten thousand. Of course, you better be damn sure you can sell forty thousand books. As a matter of fact, you better hope you can sell even ten thousand. The trick, the real art, is figuring out how much to invest in which book and when.

During the rewrites for this book, my editor asked in the margin why the above section is important to prospective authors. A fair question, to be sure. Does a writer *need* to know the ugly details of a book sale? Arguably not. What a prospective author does need to know is what publishers and agents are thinking when they reject books. Every new title is an investment and the odds of recouping that investment are not favorable. Writers need to know that their best shot at aiding the process is to write the best book they can and act professionally so as to inspire trust.

---

30. You Do Not Understand the Game of Managed Risk

Risk is a sexy word but in this case it has been co-opted by accountants. Managed risk is bean-counter lingo for determining how little you can invest in something to achieve maximum profit over the shortest amount of time. A variable-based formula, slightly different from house to house, is used to calculate how many units (see!) have to ship to cover costs and make a profit in a timely fashion. Many of the variables are easy, like figuring how much it costs to print fifteen thousand copies of a seventy-five-thousand-word manuscript on forty-pound paper in trade paperback size with a die-cut cover and French flaps. Add the cost of sales and production and you come up with a unit cost. If it calculates to be two dollars a copy with the internal shipping—sending books to various warehouses and offices—and minimum promotional copies, and the like, and you price the book at fourteen dollars with 50 percent going to the discount, there are five dollars left. Take a couple bucks for overhead, because somebody is paying for the Post-it notes and fluorescent lighting, and three bucks remain. A buck goes to the pesky author. Two dollars per copy are left over for profit. Nice tidy profit, right? Fifteen thousand copies at two dollars each equals thirty large. Do that two hundred times a year and you have six million dollars in mad money to hire Ozzy Osbourne to play the staff Christmas party.

Don't book him yet. Some annoying X-factors remain, like how do you know your book will sell fifteen thousand copies? How do you know it won't sell five thousand copies? Or five hundred? What if you print fifteen thousand copies and it sells only five thousand? Instead of thirty thousand dollars, you have ten, and you still have the costs of producing fifteen thousand units with no sales to cover the cost. What if the author or his agent wants their share up front, the full fifteen thousand dollars, nonreturnable, thank you very much. What if the author or his agent wants more because someone else is willing to pay it? What if the book does not get reviewed and nobody hears about it? What if the cost of letting people know about the book, promotions and advertising, cut too deep into the profit?

In short, how do you know how many copies will sell without a crystal ball? Thankfully, the CPAs have an answer.

31. You Do Not Understand the Soft Science of the Profit-and-Loss Statement

Visiting San Francisco for a wedding, an up-and-coming editor from a big New York house popped in to visit. We were talking books and whatnot when she brought up a term I had never heard, something called a P&L. I asked her what a P&L was and she looked at me like I had just said I had never heard of income taxes or parking tickets. Finally, convinced I was not pulling her leg, she briefly described the document to me as I made sure my office door was closed, lest my publisher hear tell of this evil practice. She asked me to let her know if any job openings might be coming up at the magical publishing house that does not have P&L statements.

I am blessed by not having to produce these documents, but from friends and colleagues, I have heard enough griping about the dreaded P&L to pray my publisher never learns of, or acknowledges, their existence.

The P&L is different at every publisher and even varies within different imprints of a large house. The formula of the P&L is considered proprietary and closely guarded by those who think anyone cares. Basically, it is a document containing forecasts of a book's sales and revenue-generating potential.

An editor who wants to acquire a book is asked to gather whatever hard data there are—the author's previous sales, for example—and mix them up with some soft data—the sales of similar books—and then add a little instinct about book reviewers' opinions, booksellers' enthusiasm, and public reaction. Put the data in a form and add up the columns to see if the best- and worst-case scenarios make the reward worth the risk. Pass the paper around at meetings to see if everyone agrees or disagrees.

When large dollar amounts are in question, ask them to stake their career, or at least the immediate forward advancement of it, on their best guesstimate.

32. You Do Not Understand Comparable Titles

The weakest link in a P&L is the comparable title. The editor is asked to list a few books, similar in subject matter and style, and base potential sales of one title on the actual sales of some others. I guess the thinking is, if you liked *Moby-Dick,* you will like other books about mad seamen and deadly whales. If you liked *Gone with the Wind,* you will love any book whose heroine is a selfish slave owner. I hope I am exaggerating the practice and I am sure it must work somehow even though it seems to have more peril than merit.

The danger in relying on comparable titles is it hinders the publication of anything unique or original. MacAdam/Cage had a commercial and critical success with a wonderful little book titled *Ella Minnow Pea: A Progressively Lipogramatic Epistolary Fable* (get thee to the OED), a book twenty publishers had turned down. When the book turned into a surprise commercial and critical success, I received several calls from editors I did not know asking for shipping and sales figures so they could use the book as a comp. One editor told me he had been sitting on a quirky book for a year hoping an anomaly would spring up so he could make a legitimate case for publication.

Warning: Do not try and help an agent or editor by suggesting comparable titles until they are already on board. If an agent has signed you and is ready to submit your manuscript, it is all right to mention some lesser-known titles that did well. If an editor is on the fence, gently supplying them with a little extra ammunition will not hurt. But as a rule, keep comparables out of your submission. If you mention a couple of bestsellers, then no one will take you seriously. Many cover letters have been made absurd by the writer saying things like *My book is a cross between* The Hunt for Red October *and* Beowulf. Leave the cross-between/blank-meets-blank game to movie producers. Besides, you do not have access to accurate sales figures or a real comparable's publishing history, so it lacks usefulness. It is best not to mention comps or P&Ls; you might look like an industry stalker. It is enough just to know the process your submission will go through.

33. You Do Not Understand the Agent Connection

Agents are much like defense attorneys, maligned by all until they need one. The worst things you have heard about agents are true: They are power-mad fiends, self-absorbed cutthroats, and turncoats. The best things you have heard about agents are also true: They are champions, advocates, counselors, coaches, and therapists. They can be all these things simultaneously.

For publishers, the main job of an agent is to be a filter. Agents find the material and we buy it from them because it is cheaper and easier than finding it ourselves. It is not very romantic, but it is true. Some agents command more respect and higher advances because publishers believe if they do not move fast and pay a lot, someone else will. Agents exploit this fear on their client's behalf. If the publisher pays a great deal for a book, then they are more likely to work hard to make sure it sells. If it sells well, the agent can repeat the process on the next book for even more money. Generally, high-powered agents like to calculate a rough estimate of what the publisher made on the first book and demand the same amount plus a nice percentage on top for the rights to acquire the next book. If the publisher does not pay, the agent moves the author to another house that benefits from groundwork laid by the first publisher. It can get ugly, but if you are the author, who cares? (I say all this for effect, knowing many authors and agents have great loyalty to publishers.)

Agents are a means by which a writer becomes an author and an author becomes a full-time author who might become a very comfortable full-time author. I accept this now, though I did not always. I have advocated for a return to the publishing practice wherein authors go directly to publishing houses and are treated well. *We—authors and publishers alike—can rid ourselves of the sycophants and return to the glory days of an artistic/commercial partnership,* I would shout into the wind. While I have toned down the rhetoric, I still believe publishers can, and should, do more to find authors themselves. But agents are here to stay and they are more than a necessary evil. They can be a very good influence on publishing and are helpful in getting books in the hands of readers, critics, and booksellers. That said, here is my favorite joke:

How many agents does it take to screw in a light bulb?
Five. Four to hold the editor down and one to screw it in.

For all my bluster, it should be noted that, although I could have attempted to sell this book by myself, I opted to go with an agent and I am glad I did, if for no other reason than I now have someone to listen to me whine at four in the morning. (Which I'm going to continue to do as soon as I find out what her new phone number is.) I was lucky. I see many agents in action and approached the one I felt was right for me.

You do not need me to tell you what an agent can do for a writer because you know. So let's get to it.

---

34. You Do Not Understand Advances

One thing all writers can agree on is big advances, when given to them, are great. Big advances given to other authors are a shameless waste of money. The question I hear more often than any other is "How do I find an agent?" and that is really a way of asking "How do I get a big fat advance?" without seeming crass. When I am asked, *How do I get a big advance?* I usually look left and right furtively, lean into their ear, and whisper, *I'm glad you asked because I've been dying to tell someone the secret. Meet me on level 3C of the underground parking garage across the street at midnight and I'll tell you. Hold a red carnation in your teeth and don't tell anyone else where you're going. Bring a pad of paper, a No. 2 pencil, and two gallons of V-8. I'll explain later.* Nobody has fallen for it yet, but someday, someone will be waiting around in the dark with some very high hopes and an awful lot of vegetable juice.

The surefire way to get a big advance is to write the right book. Then simply get the right agent to submit it at the right time to the right editor with the right marketplace. You truly control only one element of the equation and that is what you should focus on, but I am under no illusion that will satisfy anyone. So . . .

The advance is a royalty payment made before the book earns any royalties. When the book starts selling, the publisher retains the author's share of the cover price until it earns out—meaning equaling the advance amount. If you get a five-thousand-dollar advance with a royalty rate of 10 percent of the twenty-dollar cover price, you must sell twenty-five hundred copies before you earn out and start getting royalty checks. This may seem obvious, but I know a couple of authors who thought the advance was some type of bonus in addition to royalties.

To minimize the risk of their investment, editors want to pay the least amount of money for a book up front. Ideally, they would give an advance based conservatively on what the book will earn in a reasonable amount of time.

But it is not an ideal world. There is a counterintuitive school of thought: Paying little for a book is a good way to ensure that no one within the house, like the marketing and sales people, pays any attention to it, the thinking being, *If it's so great, why was it so cheap?* Whereas paying a lot is a great way to start the buzz in the industry and get in-house support by forcing the powers that be to invest in the book's promotion in order to recoup its investment—often at the expense of the rest of the titles on the list. Any editor with this in mind knows he will be blamed if the book tanks, so the fear of being a dog mitigates the temptation to be a pig.

Evilness aside, the way big advances work is fairly simple.

There are only two scenarios where the big bucks come out: the preemptive strike and the auction. Both situations require a smart agent, an exceptional manuscript, a scared or determined editor, and good timing.

The preemptive purchase, or preempt, occurs when an editor reads a manuscript and runs around the publishing house like Chicken Little saying they are going to lose the book if they do not come up with a fat offer before the agent sends the manuscript around to other houses or sets a date for an auction. The editor makes her case and is given approval to offer a load of cash on a take-it-or-leave-it basis with a tight deadline. Protocol dictates that agents cannot shop a preempt—that is, they cannot let other editors know the amount tendered in hopes they can raise more money. The agent often accepts the offer rather than risk sending it out to other houses only to have the reaction be less than receptive. It is not unheard of to have the agent and author pass on a preemptive offer and have an auction end at a figure considerably lower than what they turned down.

---

35. You Do Not Understand the Auction

An auction is exactly what it sounds like. The agent alerts several editors to a property and stokes the embers of interest into an inferno of lust. An offer, not high enough to be a preempt, comes in and the agent alerts everyone else who is considering the manuscript that they have a day or two to jump aboard. Or, if the time is right, the agent sets a specific day for all interested parties to send in their offers. The highest offer becomes the first bid and editors decide whether to go higher. The agent starts calling everybody round-robin style until there is a winner—the editor with the last, and highest, offer. Sometimes an editor will try to preempt while the auction is going on, coming in with a much higher bid than the current price, but most agents reject these because everyone else gets pissed off. Agents do, however, make hay by telling everyone else the size of the offer they just turned down, inspiring the editors to get more money approved by the higher-ups. Every blue moon, there is a tie where two houses have made the same offer and neither will increase its bid. When this happens, the agent asks the houses to submit more detailed marketing plans and other incentives to tip the balance in their favor. This is called a beauty contest.

During an auction, the higher the bids, the more attention it gets from the bigwigs at corporate houses. They even read the book if there is time. As the money increases, the interest becomes frenzied. Nobody wants to drop out because, if everyone wants the book bad enough to invest such funds, it must be a sure thing. Lacking any other quantifiable data, there is only competition. If someone else wants it, it validates your wanting it. If they will pay more than you, it makes you want it more.

Advances, it should be noted, are often a misnomer. The larger the advance, the more it is sectioned up and delivered at various milestones on the road toward and beyond publication. This is called the payout and it is usually negotiated up front. For example, a hundred-thousand-dollar advance might be divided into four payments: one on the signing of the contract, one when the manuscript has been delivered and accepted—meaning turned in with the editor's comments and criticisms satisfied, one installment on the publication of the hardcover edition, and another installment either six months later or on the publication of the paperback edition. It is not unusual for up to three years to pass before the author gets his whole advance, even longer if the book was sold on proposal.

More bad news: Advances are considered untaxed income and you get an IRS 1099 form, which means you have to set some of it aside for The Man. It is not okay to consider book advances the same as a paycheck advance, just a loan on future earnings that will be taxed later. I checked.

---

36. You Do Not Understand the Author's Role in Publishing

The good news is you do not need to know much about publishing. Your primary job is to write a great book. While you will have other duties as an author, none are more important than the stewardship you provide on the editorial level. It is really not your job to sell books. Nothing goads me more than an author who asks how many units have shipped. There are plenty of people out there referring to and thinking of your books as units. You are the author, not the sales manager. Ask questions and lend a hand, by all means, but do not forget your role.

Sometimes the best thing an author can do is back off. Let your agent and editor act as your advocates. You are not the high school football coach coming up with a winning strategy and game plan. You are not the team captain calling the plays. You are the ball, vital but inert. You should not give orders or chime in constantly on matters you know nothing about. The priority is the *book,* not the *author.* You are the main beneficiary of many people's efforts, but that does not mean they are your underlings. Your book's publicist is not your publicist. The marketing people are not your minions. They are not there to fulfill your wishes and dreams unless they coincide with the book's success. Do not ask them to chase down leads only you think are important and do not ask them to handle little chores you want done but not enough to do yourself. If you demand to call all the shots, then self-publish. If you want to tell people how to push your book, arrange to hire your own publicist. Most publishers do not mind but they also do not want the P.R. flack getting in the way.

Clearly, I am jumping the gun with this section, but knowing the rules of decorum might stop you from exhibiting signs of being high-maintenance during the submission route, particularly if the publisher is on the fence about whether or not to buy your book.

37. You Do Not Understand Publicity, Promotion, and Marketing

Publicity, promotion, and marketing are not synonymous. Publicity is coverage of the book or author—including feature stories, interviews, and reviews—and is usually the direct result of promotion, which is everything done to create publicity and shape opinion. Marketing is the same as promotion, but directed inward, toward the industry of bookselling rather than the general public. Again, it is the author's job to aid in these tasks, not direct them, because the marketplace is queer and constantly changing. When approaching agents and editors, it is understood you will work to promote your own book. Saying you are willing to tour or appear on *Oprah* is a given.

The publisher is there to sell books, which has the bonus effect of benefiting you financially and raising your literary and public profile, but that does not mean it is all about you. Even if the marketing plan is based on touting you as an author, or your personal story or particular expertise, it still is not about you. None of this means people do not want your ideas or care what your opinion is; it means we have a job to do and the worst thing an author can do is step in and distract or diminish our efforts. A good editor/publisher is conscious of the author's interests—financially, professionally, and personally. Good authors, in kind, self-check to make sure they are not becoming a pain in the ass.

I cannot count the times I have heard from other editors how their authors are driving them nuts by insisting on spending time and money on things that will not sell books. It puts them in the awkward position of either wasting money and time or angering an author. Editors, agents, and promotion and marketing people want you to be happy and have all your expectations met. The most probable way for this to happen is for you to have high hopes and realistic expectations.

Advocate for your share of promotional opportunities by being attentive and informed, but remember: Not all books on a list receive equal treatment. Some get more marketing emphasis, promotion, and review attention, and more advertising and touring money. That is the way it works at almost every house and for a very good reason: It's the best way to stay in business and grow.

I apologize for sounding like a cold-blooded prick, but it is important. Every book, no matter what the advance or first printing, is a big investment. With the printing, promotions, ads, galleys, and mailings, the cost, without overhead, is usually more than fifty thousand dollars. Making such a large investment pay off is a difficult task in the best of circumstances. Do not make it harder.

PART FOUR

THE OTHER PUBLISHING GAME

Through impatience or ignorance, you have fallen into the trap of the other publishing industry—the industry that raises your hopes, takes your money, and severely damages your chances of legitimate publishing.

38. You Fell for Self-Publishing Hype

      Life is easier if you are a cynic; I highly recommend it. You are rarely shocked, get to be right a lot, and save money on lottery tickets. Most writers are not cynics—at least not starting out. Most writers think they can change the world, or at least a little part of it. By and large, they know the odds are unfavorable, but they believe, hope, and/or know they can beat them. As any Vegas pit boss can attest to, someone who thinks they can beat the odds is ripe for the plucking, which is where the red-headed stepchild of publishing, self-publishing—formerly known as the vanity press—comes in.

As long as there have been writers with money, there have been people willing to take it. Today's vanity press has many faces. Some are cooperatives, where the author picks up a certain percentage of the production fees. Some are print-on-demand publishers, where a copy is not produced until someone orders it. Some are straightforward vanity houses, where they print the book and make it available for sale, should anyone want a copy, or ship it straight to you for distribution and marketing. A few print the book and ship it to the author at a huge markup.

The vanity press industry is extremely good at marketing and constantly reinvents itself. It is no longer vanity publishing, which sounds, well, vain. Now it is self-publishing. Recent companies have touted new technologies to make themselves seem like innovators instead of profiteers. Print on demand, where your book is spit out of a photocopierish machine and given a perfect binding (a flat spine, glued along the inside edge), was pushed as a revolution where every book in the world would be available at any bookstore no matter how small. *Yours could be one of the first,* they told writers. But POD has not caught on yet with bookstores or consumers. Other self-publishing houses tout their national distribution, meaning any bookstore is allowed to order your book, even though they most likely will not. Sometimes the printers make you commit to a certain number of copies being sold. You pay for bad cover design and cheap binding. You pay to participate in marketing programs, which are weak at best. You will have the opportunity to participate in cooperative advertising—whence you and other dupes chip in together for an advertisement, with the vanity house getting a cut above the ad's cost. You pay for all the bells and whistles they can think of. They take no risk on you. The more you believe in your book, the more money they make.

Is the vanity press a scam? Kind of. But it is not necessarily fraud. Clients generally get what they pay for, but what you are paying for is not much despite how it is packaged. You pay to produce copies of your book and share any profits with the printer.

Oddly, vanity printing is the genesis of today's publishing. Two and three hundred years ago, almost all books were produced using the author's, or his family's and friends', money. The bookseller took a cut and the author got the rest. This changed with the advent of modern publishing in the early part of the twentieth century, when royalty structures were established and the advance system was born. Bookselling and publishing became industrialized and profitable. Agents soon followed.

Sadly, my mother is an optimist who often believes what she is told until she learns otherwise. I learned this years ago as a grade school student, when my mother raced out of the living room and implored me to give her the phone. I figured something was on fire or one of my many siblings was drowning again. She dialed a number she had scratched into her palm with, I think, a pair of cuticle scissors. It was an 800 number. I listened as she read off her Visa number to an operator who, luckily, was standing by. Mom put down the phone relieved and I asked her what she had just ordered. "A video recording camera," she beamed. "Now we can put our family memories on something called Beta and enjoy them for years." "What was the rush?" I demanded. "If I didn't call in the next five minutes," she said, "I wouldn't have gotten the free carrying case."

When the box arrived, months later, it contained a large plastic video camera weighing only six ounces. Turns out the camera needed to be plugged into a VCR—which we did not have—in order to actually record something. While the plastic camera quickly became a white elephant, my mother did make use of the carrying case for an overnight bag. She is probably still making payments on it. (And the memories? They are lost forever, except the ones I retain for comedic embellishment.)

My favorite vanity presses are for poetry anthologies. They offer to publish your poem for no charge; they even give out a big prize for the best work of verse in the anthology. The downside is you have to buy a copy, or copies, of the book for some ungodly sum. My ten-year-old sister, who learned about the "poetry competition" from a teacher (!) who was sent a flyer, fell for this, and my mother, as expected, jumped right on board. Her poem, and twenty thousand others, appeared unedited in the smallest typeface available for no one at all to see. She did not win the prize.

Optimists suffer. They get their hopes dashed and their wallets emptied. Look at late-night television. Hundreds of ads promise a brighter tomorrow. If you stay up late and have a credit card, you can be assured of no-risk opportunities for three easy payments. Pascal was right, we want to be deceived. We will take the enticing lie over the obvious truth every time.

Why? Because we really, really want to. The truth does not sell very well. It is an ugly, sweaty thing requiring work and discipline. We want to believe there is an electrical device that, when strapped onto our love handles, will give us a meaty abdominal six-pack even while sitting on our fat asses eating Milk Duds. We do not like the truth because it is simple, we do not want the truth because it is hard, and we do not trust the truth because it is free.

Perhaps because many are idealists and publishing is so frustrating, writers are particularly vulnerable to believing in those who offer hope in exchange for cash. Writers know life is tough and we all want to think of an easier way. Maybe for a rare few, there is. If you count on that, you are a chump and somebody is going to take your money and break your heart. Or you are going to end up with a plastic camera and monthly payments.

39. You Think Self-Publishing Will Get You Taken More Seriously

The vanity press's target audience is the dejected, frustrated, and impatient writer. Its sales pitch is designed to pander to his ego, laziness, and sense of self-defeat. But—like all effective sales pitches—vanity presses make it seem otherwise. These imprints take out ads in glossy magazines touting your new power to publish, free from the publishing industry's shackles of elitism and fecklessness. The ads proudly bellow:

The problem's not you or your book, it's *Them*. They are a bunch of elitist snobs holed up in New York high-rises ignoring your certain bestseller. *They* don't know a great book when they see it. Who needs *Them*. You are now in control. You call the shots. *(Please make the check or money order out to Vanity Books Inc.)*

The whole thing sounds very American. You are not a reject, you are a rebel. You are not a loner, you are an individualist. You are your own man and no one but you controls your destiny.

You have the control because you have the cash. Most everyone I have talked to who has self-published with a vanity house was disappointed, some very much so. The production of a book is the easy part, it is the distribution and marketing that is hard; the vanity press has no easy, or cheap, solution for getting your books into stores or getting it reviewed. Most newspaper and magazine book review sections do not review self-published books and most wholesalers, which account for the majority of bookstore orders, will not stock the vanity titles.

Even if money does not matter, self-publishing can hurt a writer's career. After a writer has grown impatient with a manuscript and has it self-published, she is usually disappointed with the results and starts submitting it to publishing houses.

When a submission comes in the form of a self-published book, it most often tells an editor the book was submitted everywhere and turned down. So the author self-published and tried marketing it herself and it failed to break out. This does not instill confidence and we usually do not take it seriously.

There are, by design of course, exceptions. If there were not, fewer people would be fooled. Every time I rail against vanity publishing, someone brings up *Chicken Soup for the Soul* and all its schlocky spawn. True, the series grew from a self-published book to a cottage industry to a multi-million-dollar brand. This is the rare, if not singular, exception and I do not think its success will ever be repeated. *Chicken Soup* is an unwitting accomplice in fleecing well-intentioned, but impatient, authors. I would bet that for every dollar the *Chicken Soup* guys made, other writers lost ten.

Under certain circumstances, a vanity title will be looked at carefully or even republished by a legitimate press if it wins an award or does unusually well in the market. I know of several instances when a writer self-published one early book only to have a later one find its way into standard publishing with the publisher reissuing the vanity title. There are certainly a few instances when self-publishing makes sense. The vanity press is a good forum for family and small-town histories, extremely niche markets like people who collect lint and revisionist historians, and getting Grandma's bodice ripper into print before her passing. If you are not really interested in doing the work necessary to be legitimately published, and want a copy to bandy about at cocktail parties, then go with self-publishing. Only do it knowing what to expect.

Generally, self-publishing is a waste of time and money. Anytime you are writing a check, there is a chance you are being taken to the cleaners—and that likelihood is lessened only by the amount of research you have done beforehand and the amount of common sense you apply to the situation. As with many things, if something sounds like an easy shortcut to your dreams, then it is suspect at best. At the risk of being repetitive, getting published is very hard and there are no shortcuts for sale to get you there.

40. You Signed with a Pay-to-Play Agent

Like most people, I learn very important lessons only by doing very stupid things.

When MacAdam/Cage was starting out, we researched book production, marketing, and distribution and felt comfortable with running the business; but finding the titles to publish was vexing. While we started getting submissions from eagle-eyed writers shortly after setting up shop, we assumed agents represented all the great books. After sending every agent in the country a letter announcing our existence and noble intentions, I cleared considerable shelf space for the deluge of literary offerings sure to follow. We were answered by an underwhelming trickle.

One agency, however, began sending a hoard of material. Every week, a meaty package would arrive teeming with short descriptions of books, usually one paragraph, in every genre and subject matter. Being a naïf, and, admittedly, fairly stupid, I thought they must have read our letter of introduction and become enthusiastic about our bold little venture.

From the number of titles they represented, I assumed they were a big agency. I read their laundry list, and requested several titles to review. I was surprised when the vast majority turned out to be very bad, but I remained undeterred. Finally, one popped out that I loved. My publisher concurred and I called to make an offer. I should have been tipped off by the surprise in the agent's voice. He did not quite know what to do. He agreed to my first offer and I felt like quite the shrewd little negotiator.

For a time, all was well. The contracts were signed, the author was a dream to work with, and the book was shaping up nicely. Then cracks started to form.

I began to see through the fog after talking to the author one day shortly after signing the contract. He mentioned how happy he was to have found a house because he was having serious doubts about his agent—after all the money the author had paid to the agent, he was beginning to think it was a racket.

That is when he told me he had given the agent several sizable payments over many months for representing the book. Worse, the agent was horrible about returning the author's calls. When they did speak, the author became convinced the agent had not read the book. My brow furrowed until my contact lenses popped out. I recalled my conversations with the agent and remembered that every time I started to talk about editing the book, he tilted the conversation toward his love of boating. At the time, I just thought he was a bore, in the way only yachtsmen can be, but now I was catching on to something more sinister. I began an exhaustive investigation (actually, I typed the agent's name into a search engine) and found an entire community of former clients and writers devoted to exposing the seafaring fraud and others of his ilk.

The most concerning hit I received was the agent's own Web site, which was littered with references about the book sale to our house. He was using our name (we had recently garnered some good press) to hook more fish. Furthermore, the critical Web sites had picked up on this and were painting us with the same brush as Commodore Rip-Off.

If I had done the most rudimentary bit of research, I would have found out whom I was dealing with ahead of time. I still would have read the submissions, if for no other reason than it was virgin hunting ground, because every other house was staying away. But I would have known to control the agent's use of our name, and make him revise his author agreement to industry standards and give back the money our author had paid him.

Sometimes vanity agents are easy to sniff out because they are pure money hogs, sucking you dry of every dollar you are willing to invest in your dream. They start with a small fee, usually a few hundred dollars up front for postage, then hook you in for more by referring you to a sham editing service or book doctor, who kicks back money to the agent. Then they hit you for more fees, perhaps monthly, to widen the submission circle because you are so close and every rejection has been a near miss.

They do submit your book, just not in a way that works for editors: with a separate cover letter, a call before and after it is sent, and the laborious but necessary follow-up. They do not build relationships with editors, investigate new markets, or follow industry trends. They merely submit the book in short form, doing just enough to fill any contractual obligation so you cannot sue them or break the contract. Ick.

Most often, there is more gray than black and white. Some smaller agencies, particularly newer ones, charge small reading fees, usually refundable upon signing of a representation agreement, and postage fees to cover mailing costs. Some charge large reading fees. While I understand the burdens of starting a business, I think it is wrong. The agent should be the first investor in a writer's career and should take risk on his behalf. Besides, relative to small-business start-up costs, a literary agency is cheap. Many agencies have been started with a laser printer and a library card. To take money from clients to ensure even minimal expenses are not out-of-pocket smacks of the untoward. My agent disagrees with me on this point, saying though charging for time is wrong, passing on some hard costs to the author after a book sale makes sense. I do not think she would appreciate the publisher passing on hard costs to authors, even after the book makes money. But deducting mailing and Xerox costs from royalty checks is a normal practice for agents and is unlikely to change. Reading fees, however, are not industry standard and are vehemently frowned on by all reputable agents.

This does not mean all fee-charging agents are con artists, at least not starting out. Some probably never felt financially comfortable enough to stop charging or do not see a reason to if people are willing to pay. Here is why it is wrong: Artists should not pay, not for a hired gun posing as an advocate. Artists can pay to learn and improve their craft. They can pay for their materials and experiences, even to promote their work; but they cannot pay to have someone be their champion. What the creator needs is a hopeful or even faithful believer, not a mercenary.

You would be surprised how many people, overcome with relief and excitement, sign whatever contract is put in front of them and are happy to write a check. How do you avoid the vanity agent scam? By using basic common sense and by trusting your instincts:

- Check out the agent at writing Web sites like www.anotherrealm.com/prededitors/ and www.publishersmarket place.com.
- Google him.
- Check with the Association of Artists' Representatives to see if he is a member or on a "beware of" list.
- Check his résumé to see if he has ever sold a book.
- Ask to talk to some of his clients who have been published and some who have yet to be published.

So you know, the standard agency commission is 15 percent and should have a thirty- to sixty-day termination clause. The agency agreement should not include the "option book," the subsequent title to the one being submitted or sold, meaning, if he sells your book and you part ways, the agent is still commissioned on your next book.

41. You Go to Writers' Conferences for the Wrong Reasons

I am a bit nervous about biting the hand that feeds me in this section because I go to many conferences as a "faculty member" and am treated warmly: given a generous per diem, free drinks, and often a nice tote bag full of swag. I generally have a good time and people nod their heads thoughtfully when I answer a question, even when I don't make any sense. It's nice.

Although I want to continue being asked to attend, I have some concerns about the explosion of writers' conferences around the country and who is paying for my club sandwiches and tote bags . . . and why.

The idea of getting writers together with more established authors, agents, and editors to give advice and encouragement is a good one. It is a fine way for the successful to share wisdom and experience with others just starting out or on the wrong path. There is also a great sense of community building, where writers feel they are becoming part of something, making them more confident and productive.

However, I wonder at what point it becomes redundant and even wasteful or distracting. I have met the same man at three conferences in three states; I thought he was a stalker until I realized he did not even recognize me, having had so many advisers over the years. The last time I met him he had the same book under his arm he had the first time with no revisions I could discern. I could brush him off as an anomaly if I did not keep getting query letters from unpublished writers touting all the conferences they have attended as if having a free weekend and a thousand dollars is a publishing credential akin to publishing a short story.

Ballsier are those who claim to have studied under renowned authors after spending two hour-long sessions with them over a weekend at a ski resort with thirty other people. While such brief encounters may be meritorious, they belittle those who spent two years working with the same author getting a postgraduate degree. Though I am all in favor of putting the shiny side of the apple out, you have to be careful of crossing the line into misrepresentation. Writers need to tell the truth. Leave the hyperbole to your agent.

I am also concerned with the structure of writers' conferences and the mix of writing seminars to help people build strong characters, improve their plots, even find a subject for a book before the lunch break, followed by how to get published or find an agent after the lunch break. What the heck are people doing during lunch to make them ready for a move from one to the other?

I think writers' conferences are great in many ways, such as motivating writers and giving them a morale boost. Like anything, they can be abused. The ideal candidates for a conference are writers and authors with completed manuscripts who are fairly confident they have done all they can in preparation to debut the manuscript in the cutthroat arena of a writing workshop. Everyone should have a completed manuscript unless they are committed to being a professional short-story writer (good luck!) or they have written a proposal on a nonfiction topic that cannot become an entire manuscript without an advance. Someone who is flirting with the idea of writing a book or who is a couple of chapters in is throwing her money away, wasting her time, and risking misdirection by getting ahead of herself.

In my world, a writers' conference would emulate scientific conferences, with people delivering detailed papers on such topics as:

- Internal dialogue: Italics or quotation marks?
- Character duality: Three views . . . or not.
- Multiple points of view: One man's perspective.
- Is it still magical realism if no one cares?

Part of me thinks writers' conferences (and M.F.A. programs, for that matter) would be more valuable if attendees, and some faculty, were forced to attend a class on sentence diagramming. Maybe even a double session on using a comma and leaving *s* off the end of the word *toward*.

Perhaps this ideal writers' conference should be separated from its unmentioned-but-more-valued conjoined twin—the how-to-find-an-agent-and-get-a-big-advance conference. No one would go to the former. And I wouldn't get a tote bag.

42. You Found the Wrong Book Doctor or Editing Service

This one is easy. You do not need a book doctor—with two exceptions. The first is if a reputable agent, and I mean beyond reproach, refers you to a book doctor because your book is getting a lot of near-miss rejections. Even then, the fixer should not be a client of the agent so there is no temptation to get a commission on the agent's failure. The second exception is if you are a nonwriter (a CEO, doctor, lawyer) writing a book in your field but you lack the skills to impart your information clearly.

Otherwise, you are paying someone to do what is your responsibility. If your book is in trouble, learn how to fix it, then fix it. Do not pay someone to do your job for you. If you do, then you are not a writer, just a contractor. Besides, I cannot believe a book doctor will care about your vision nearly as much as you do. If it gets published, you will not feel like it is yours.

Another exception might be if you have been writing the book for a long time and are convinced you have become too close to your own material to have any objectivity and the frustration level is becoming dangerously high. If you feel you are a good candidate in need of a freelance editor, do your homework and research them thoroughly. Look for one who has had good results after publication and has many references from happy clients. Perhaps start with a tryout of fifty pages before committing to the entire project as most freelancers work by the hour or by the project, depending on what the writer is comfortable with.

That being said, I will doctor anyone's book for $28,752.49. Really. I swear to God. Everyone has a price. That's mine.

43. You Listened to Some Bad Advice

Ambrose Bierce, the patron saint of cynics, defined *advice* in *The Devil's Dictionary* as "n. The smallest current coin." Advice in the writing trade is as common as ditch water. Countless books, magazines, and Web sites proffer tactics, tidbits, and tricks on getting published. Some of it is good and some of it is garbage. So how do you know if a piece of advice is sound? As a rule, good advice usually smacks of common sense and usually entails some hard work.

Bad advice is expensive and sounds like music to your ears. So listen to your own common sense, keep focused, and beware of hucksters peddling too-good-to-be-true schemes. There may be a few shortcuts here and there, but actively seeking them out is a mistake. It is best to focus on fundamentals and leave theatrics to those whose writing cannot stand alone.

Some of the worst advice I have heard about writing and publishing follows:

- *Do not let someone tell you no.*

There is a philosophy of tenacity for getting what you want. The don't-take-no-for-an-answer mantra is usually espoused by salesman types who try and turn lambs into lions through motivational tapes and whatnot. I cannot speak for other industries, but it does not work in publishing. When a manuscript is rejected and the author tries different tactics to appeal the decision, such as sending the book directly to the publisher with a note saying the editor has made a mistake, the writer has burned his bridge with the house for good.

Some writers who have been near misses at literary agencies and publishers get it in their heads they can reverse a decision by campaigning. They find thin excuses to call or write with an update on their careers—a poem published in their college alumni newsletter or some mysterious movie producer they met while flying coach said their book would make a great movie. This contact may feel like diligence to the writer, but it comes across as haranguing.

• *Find current publishing trends and write to break in.*

Since Harry Potter and Lemony Snicket, many writers have turned away from adult fiction and started producing fantastical young-adult novels in droves. That is fine, if they have a passion for that subject matter. Writing in different genres is great; it allows a writer to exercise all her literary muscles and can keep her out of a rut. If the motivation is to have a more marketable product, the work will reflect that and the result will be a complete waste of time. Publishing is cyclical, genres and fetishes move in and out of favor, but there is always a market for a great book in any area. Trying to write to the market is a fool's errand. Do not write a legal thriller if your passion is gritty short stories. A *Dummies* guide will not lead you to *War and Peace*. Your best chance of getting published is by submitting what you love, not what publishers and agents want to see.

• *Show some panache by making your submission stand out.*

I swear this does not work. Do not send your book in with any fresh-baked food products. Do not fill the submission envelope with glitter. Do not send your manuscript in via singing telegram or male stripper. (If you are intent on adding something to your submission, a bottle of fine single-malt scotch is a classic.) Only once, in years of witnessing some of the wackiest ideas brought to bear, have I been impressed by a writer's trick to gain extra attention. I read some of his book, wrote a short rejection, stuffed it into the return SASE, and sent it off. It came back to the office because the SASE was actually addressed to me. I thought the author was an idiot until I saw a small notation below the address reading "Right back at ya." The book was called *Boomerang*.

———

Now might be a good time to tell you this: I am not an expert on the publishing industry. I have some limited influence on my own little sliver and I pay as close attention to what is going on in the industry as I can stomach. Everything I have written is what I think is right based on my experiences and a different editor might have a completely different perspective. As with anything important, the final word on what works rests with you, the writer.

Counsel is relative. If some advice seems wrong for your book, it probably is. Trust yourself as the guardian of your own career—after you feel confident you know everything you need to know to be a good judge.

PART FIVE

SLUSH DIVING

Blindly sending your book out to agents and editors will land you in the slush pile, and the chances of getting out are slim.

44. You Will Rot in the Slush Pile as the Publishing House's Lowest Priority

Writers assume if they do not have an agent or a professional referral to an editor, they will end up in the fabled Slush Pile. This assumption is correct.

The slush pile is a legendary beast in publishing lore, for agents, editors, and especially writers. For writers, it is a guardian of the gates to the golden city, utterly unforgiving and seemingly invincible. For agents, the slush is an ever-growing chore. For publishers, it is a monster, capable of growing out of control and taking up all available office space if not dealt with occasionally.

With few exceptions, every author has spent some time in a slush pile. The annals of publishing are filled with stories of now-celebrated authors who amassed enough rejection slips to use as an ottoman. Going over the transom is a rite of passage.

Most slush piles today are composed of samples, usually the first three chapters, a cover letter, a synopsis, and a self-addressed stamped envelope. Many large houses now refuse to accept unsolicited materials and recycle them as soon as they are received. Some cite September 11/anthrax-type concerns, but I think they just cannot be bothered.

Unsolicited manuscripts—meaning works sent by someone we do not know and have no reason to trust—are usually tossed into mail buckets or shelved in supply closets. Submissions sit there until there is a pressing need for storage space or the interns have finished alphabetizing the office supplies. Then they are glanced at before being returned with a short note expressing empty sentiments along the lines of "good luck with your future endeavors."

As a rule, literary agencies take unsolicited submissions much more seriously than publishing houses do. They read them faster and request full manuscripts sooner, and, more often than editors, give suggestions on how to improve the work. Newer or smaller agencies are generally more responsive because they often have open lists—meaning they have time to represent more people than they presently do. Sometimes, when agents reject writers, they give thoughtful advice in hopes that the writer will return with better material. Many agents, particularly those not aligned with a bicoastal, bottom-line, corporate overlord, are in the business specifically to find new voices.

Most big-name agents like to work primarily from other talent pools, like author referrals and by scouring national and prestigious literary magazines for promising or exciting new authors. A few pay as little or less attention to submissions as editors do. (I once told a top agent I met at a book convention that my house specialized in debut fiction. He sniffed and said he never handled first books. The implication being, when he wanted a client, he went out and picked someone already successful.)

There are agents of all stripes, some great, many good, and a few evil. With a few exceptions, agents and their assistants do review all their slush. This is bad news for the writer who uses the excuse of his material is not even being read when he submits it because he got a form rejection. Sorry, it is. They just do not want it—at least not yet.

I try not to call it the slush pile. I prefer the term "General Submission Pile," but not because I am afraid to hurt writers' feelings. Rather, I avoid the term because I have found authors through unsolicited submission who do not like being referred to as "from the slush pile." I can understand this. Just because they did not have a big agent or play golf with our publisher does not mean their writing is garbage. The slush pile might be the right name for general submissions after they have been gone through carefully and the gems plucked out. Of course, I often slip and refer to the constantly regenerating buckets of submissions as slush; it is hard not to sometimes. (In this book I generally use *slush* for brevity and clarity—and because it is a fun word, independent of its meaning and connotation: Sssluuuushh.)

At MacAdam/Cage, where I oversee the general-submission coverage, we do things in three parts. Submissions are collected every other day or so, and gone through briefly to remove everything that is obviously not in our publishing spectrum, such as Christian, romance, science fiction, and New Age. This generally cuts the pile in half. An intern, an assistant editor, or an editor will then review, again briefly, the remaining submissions, scanning the cover letter and reading a page or two. This reduces the stack by 90 percent. The survivors are read more extensively and the stack is reduced to a mere handful. The handful gets letters requesting the entire manuscript and the rest get a form rejection. Of the full manuscripts we request, less than 1 percent are eventually published by our house.

45. You Are Kidding Yourself If You Think You Are Not in the Slush Pile

Through pride or overconfidence, many writers do not feel their work is placed in the slush pile. They believe their credentials, the quality of their prose, and/or their storytelling abilities will instantly levitate them above the other submissions. They will call in to question their rejection slip, thinking it was a clerical error. I will politely tell them it is no error, and they will hang up—still in doubt.

Occasionally, writers think if they reach an editor or agent by phone or meet them in person, they will not be put in the slush. While sometimes true, this is certainly no guarantee. A good phone chat or pleasant meeting can help, but, unless it was exceptional, you will probably end up in the slush pile anyway. We might write a note expressing our reasons for passing on your book, but it is only a small courtesy and should not be overvalued.

Many times, a writer is completely unaware of the volume of material being sent to agents and publishers.

46. There Is Too Much Slush

The small house I work for receives about four thousand submissions a year and more than three thousand of them are unsolicited. We publish fewer than thirty books a year. Unlike many houses, we strive to take all work seriously and look at pages quickly. Still, we are constantly in danger of being overwhelmed by sample chapters and self-addressed stamped envelopes. If we get distracted and let the pile build, then dozens of boxes full of manuscripts and samples will be lined up against the walls.

The modern slush pile is Xerox's fault. The advent of photocopying meant writers could produce an unlimited number of manuscripts and send them out en masse at minimal cost. The personal computer (and printer) only made it worse. Many writers today send unsolicited queries and manuscripts via e-mail, leaving the job of printing them out or reading a large document on screen to us. Unless requested, do not do this. It makes you come across as cheap and lazy.

With word processing as the norm and even bookwriting software common, the physical act of writing is easier than ever; manuscripts are being produced at an alarming rate. Editors and agents I have talked to estimate the number of novels and memoirs written every year in this country to be between fifteen thousand and fifty thousand. Only a tiny fraction of these are published by legitimate presses—for good reason. The great majority of the slush is unpublishable, some of it is unreadable, even painful or laughable. Which means that when you're in the slush . . .

47. You Are in Bad Company

Being in the slush means you are surrounded by a lot of malodorous writing and painful dreck and you will be judged by the company you keep. You might say a good submission (yours) benefits by comparison to the bad (everyone else's), but it is not true. Reading piles of mediocre-to-lousy writing leaves a person numb, worn out, and prone to miss gems. One fresh clam will not undo the ills of a platter of bad ones.

The honor of being the worst manuscript ever submitted to MacAdam/Cage, in my opinion, was held for years by a tome whose title I suppose I should not mention. I'll call it *Love/Love* because that word appeared twice in the four-word title—not a good sign. Every sentence began with "It was" or "He was" or, for the occasional treat, "They were." The author clearly felt punctuation was an optional exercise, particularly in his many free-verse dream sequences. The story was a thinly disguised, heavily subjective account of a gifted writer's divorce from a shrill wife who quashed his gift for poetry by demanding he make a living. Examples of the "poetry" were liberally sprinkled throughout the work. (A highlight was a ditty blaming child support payments for the death of art in America.) The manuscript was so self-indulgent, smarmy, and shoddy it made my eyes bleed and I want to reject it again every time it comes to mind.

Recently, a new submission knocked *Love/Love* off the pedestal of shame. I would print the title of this work here, but the writer forgot to include it on the manuscript or in the cover letter. The writing, alternately dull and confusing, dragged on while the writer took liberties with grammar that would make a professional wrestler wince. Yoda better syntax had. The story was incomprehensible babble having something to do with wealthy, emotionally distant Canadians and a tuna boat.

It may sound like I am picking on easy targets—people trying to find a home for their pride and joy—but it is my opinion and opinion is the editor's only real tool in judging a book. We do not absolutely know very much, but we have opinions. Every editor has a story, seldom told, about declining a manuscript only to watch it land somewhere else, then achieve strong sales, great reviews, and prestigious prizes. But editors have to go with what they think, because what we know is not enough. For all I know, *Love/Love* may sell like the next *Bridges of Madison County* and the unknown manuscript could be hailed as the successor to *Finnegans Wake*.

I said earlier, I respect any writer who has the perseverance to finish a book, and I do. We always try to reject books respectfully with, if possible and appropriate, some encouragement and advice. While I may respect the effort, that does not mean I have to respect the result.

To editors, the slush pile can be a great source of caustic humor. Badly written manuscripts with asinine story lines abound. Sometimes, I will find one so delightfully bad, I feel compelled to find someone in the office to share it with. If several of the staff are going through the pile (I call it slush diving), we will pass doozies back and forth, trying to outdo each other. The best of the lot are added to a file in my office labeled simply When Hell Freezes Over. I admit, it is a cruel exercise given the good intentions of the writer in sending in her work; but without venting, the task of vetting unsolicited submissions would be tortuous.

Even given the cynical nature of slush diving, occasionally someone will come across something special. If several of us are going through the pile at the same time, one person may hold a submission longer than necessary and will go noticeably quiet. (This is usually where I come sniffing around trying to pry it from their fingers.) A submission standing out on its merits—a sharp letter, well-presented and understated, over sample chapters that entice you and do not let you go. This is a great moment.

Horrid manuscripts are not the rule. Most submissions are decently written and earnestly told stories that do not inspire love or hatred—they simply do not inspire. They are good, just not good enough to publish. Many manuscripts start off nicely and then fall apart. I remember one title about expatriates in Prague that introduced an ensemble of vivid characters facing disparate situations. The scene was lovely, the writing plain and strong, and the dialogue (possibly the toughest thing to master) believable and honest. I could not wait for the characters to all come together and meet. They did meet, in some sort of Kung Fu dojo where they all learned that the way to deal with complex emotions is to kick some Czech ass. The second part of the book was an endless string of fight descriptions. It was like the author gave a half-written book to a teenager to finish. When a book falls apart and cannot be fixed, it is heartbreaking.

When a diamond (or at least a potential diamond) is unearthed in the slush pile, I dance like a fool in the rain. I get the publisher excited, and, hopefully, I get the author excited. Do not forget, it does not happen often enough. Not nearly enough. More often than not, when it comes to the slush pile . . .

48. You Are an Uninvited Guest at the Publishing Party

When an agent or a previously published author submits something, editors pay varying degrees of attention to it based on our trust of and respect for the agent or writer.

Over time, editors and agents trust their authors and clients to know their taste and know what is publishable and sellable. Good writers are generally protective of their editors' and agents' time and refrain from recommending every acquaintance with a Smith-Corona. When these authors make a referral, we get excited. If we get a submission, we treat it seriously. We read these manuscripts in a better frame of mind. If there are flaws, we can be inclined to look past them.

But if you come in cold, we do not know you and are disinclined to believe you are the real thing. You will, most likely, not get a break in the slush pile.

Nothing in the slush gets the benefit of the doubt. Reading the slush, editors or—more likely—their assistants are biased against you. They know, even if your submission is very good, it is going to be a tough road to publication at most houses. If they decide to champion your manuscript, their coworkers and bosses are going to treat it with great skepticism and maybe even scorn. If it is so good, what is it doing in the slush? How did it get by the agents and other houses?

With more manuscripts flooding in, and staff resources at a premium, publishing houses have increased their reliance on agents in recent years to weed out the crap and submit the next big thing. Agents accept this charge gladly.

As publishers rely more on agents, we rely less on books submitted directly to the house. The agents comb the slush (and other sources) to find gems. Publishers gladly pay for the service with large advances, even though the same book might be in their storage closet at the same moment. (Editors sometimes prefer to buy from an agent even if they do not have to. See "Part Six: Agents Provocateurs.") It is the it's-too-good-to-be-true philosophy. It is ridiculous, but . . .

49. The Slush Pile, Like the Publishing Industry, Does Not Make Sense

Treating general submissions like a waste of paper seems counterintuitive. If the object of publishing is to find great books, you would think the place to start looking would be in the pile of manuscripts down the hall. If the object is to sign up books as inexpensively as possible to minimize investment, then the unagented author who would probably accept a reasonable offer without much squawking seems ideal. You may think because they can get cheaper books, more rights, and grateful authors, publishing houses would be focusing on the slush as a place to find low-risk, high-payoff projects. They are not.

Publishing is a business largely based on enthusiasm and validation. In short, it works best as follows. Big Agent finds a book on referral from Famous Client or professor at prestigious M.F.A. program and sends it to select group of Well-Thought-Of Editors who are told it is a Hot Property and the clock is ticking. Well-Thought-Of Editors make copies to pass around to other editorial colleagues, careful not to make them envious, and gather allies for an editorial meeting, if they can wait that long. Hot Property is given to Bigwigs-Who-Can-Write-Big-Checks and Sales-and-Marketing Gurus along with a profit-and-loss statement. The P&L predicts, based on sales of other books with similar themes and enthusiastic beginnings, how this book might sell in the real world. If heads are nodding at the next meeting, Bigwigs give Well-Thought-Of Editors permission to make offers. If any single offer is not big enough to take it off the table, an auction starts. The Big Agent takes the largest offer and makes it the first bid and the Editors go back to their Bosses asking for more money to bid. As the price rises, some houses reach the limit of their enthusiasm relative to their pocketbooks, so they drop out. Finally, there is the Well-Thought-Of-But-Now-Nervous Acquiring Editor on top with the best bid, the Hot Property, and a big, hopeful smile. Worried about the company's investment and his or her own job, Bigwig approves a large marketing budget, and they're off to the races.

50. Enthusiasm Does Not Come from the Slush

The enthusiasm begins with the agent, who knows both the editor's taste and what does well (or, rather, what has done well) in the marketplace. The agent generates interest with the threat of having the book sell to another house and hit the bestseller list there, leaving an editor the unpleasant task of explaining to the publisher why it is not on their list. The enthusiasm becomes interest from multiple houses, the interest becomes action in terms of an offer or offers, the action becomes validation, and the validation begets more enthusiasm and further offers. This is the model for the six-figure and sometimes seven-figure advances we hear about.

Now, if that same book is submitted over the transom and is found by the acquiring editor in the slush, the story is a bit different.

Someone reads the submission, requests the manuscript, and an editor gets to it eventually. There is no reason to rush, because no one is shopping it around. There is no agent to vouch for the author or to relay relevant but awkward-to-ascertain information (such as, is the author good-looking enough to appear on television? Is he or she related to someone famous? Is the author rich enough to help pay for the promotion of his or her own book?). Also, the editor is secretly worried about the plethora of good reasons why this book is in the slush pile (Is the author a known pederast? Is it plagiarized? Or most often: Am I the only one in the world who will like this book?).

The editor tentatively asks the boss to have a look. The editor's boss eventually reads the book and wonders why the editor is so lukewarm and says, "Let's see how the list shapes up." If the list has room, then the editor gets the green light to call the author and tender a small offer. The book is given a modest marketing budget, placing it on the house midlist where it is left to fend for itself.

Obviously, these are two extremes of an oversimplified

scenario. While stories of slush-pile books finding an audience and becoming bestsellers and winning prizes are out there, they are rare. The average acquisition story is somewhere in between these two examples, but the point remains the same: In big publishing, validation begets enthusiasm, which begets success.

Small presses, like the one I work for, tend to base their enthusiasm on personal tastes and experiences, possibly because we are in competition with other small houses, so for us, there is a rush. The lack of an agent is potentially good news because it means we can get the book for a price that will not break us or eat all our marketing money. The question of whether we are the only ones who will like the book remains until the reviews come in—but that is the job.

In publishing, as in any business where art is the product, there are efforts to quantify the marketability of taste. The results can be cruel and unjust to the artist. Every so often, the right thing happens, a great book rises to the top of the slush, an editor is enthralled, a boss is impressed, and a bigwig jumps on board with the marketing department in tow. For this to even be an option, however, the writer must do his or her job well. (Nothing can help you if your writing stinks and your book is either a bad idea well realized or a good idea poorly realized.) The submission must be near perfect in form and substance. It will never happen if . . .

51. You Missed Your First-Chance Glance

You can never forget that it is in the publishing industry's best interest to reject you, discourage you, and ignore you. We—editors and agents, big and small—have more writers than we need with more budding authors appearing every day. We form biases against submissions for the most minor offenses, including manuscripts spaced incorrectly for our sensitive eyes, bad titles, and author names too hard to pronounce out loud. (Well, maybe not the last one.) We scrunch our noses if a plot sounds farfetched or it seems similar to a book that did not do well. We reject books if the first sentence is too flat, or too purple.

Of the publishing houses that accept unsolicited submissions and the handful that treat them seriously, the majority want only a few chapters—some want as little as ten or so pages. The idea behind the minimalist approach is that we can reject based on very little and ask for more if we are intrigued. For the most part, we judge a book primarily on its cover letter. The samples are skimmed and a few pages read, but it is usually a cursory pass. (It is an encouraging sign when an entire sample is read.)

When an editor or agent (or more likely an intern or assistant) opens your submission, they briefly scan it looking for a reason not to reject it. We want to find new authors and new books. We work hard at it. We live for it. Jaded we may be, but we know every piece sent in could be the next big thing no matter how long the odds.

The quick glance given to your submission when it is

first looked at is your best chance at being taken seriously and generating enthusiasm.

The first thing we want to know is if the submission was requested and is expected. The opening usually tells us: Dear Pat, here is my manuscript, *How to Get a College Degree Without Learning to Read,* that you asked to see when we met at the Muncie Writers Festival . . . or . . . As per our phone call last month, I am sending my memoir, *Three Days in Traffic School: A Life Interrupted* . . .

Second, we want to see if the writer was referred to us: I am sending my manuscript at the request of your client Ima Moneymaker . . . or . . . Your author Juan Libro de Oro, who was in my M.F.A. program, suggested that I send my novel, *Apathy in the Time of Diphtheria,* when it was finished . . .

If these avenues are not open to you and you are sending something in without being requested or referred, there is still good news. As long as we are there, we will skim the letter to see what the book is about and who wrote it.

This is where writers commit a multitude of sins. The cover letter at most houses is a tracking document. It is shown around agencies and editorial offices. If it is a junior staffer who first reads it, it is shown to bosses. It is brought to meetings and discussed. It is the best indication of a writer to be taken seriously. Therefore, the letter has to be taken seriously by the writer.

Cover letters are almost always too long. Containing a full synopsis of the book, a "short" bio relating every event since entering high school, a myriad of marketing ideas, and uninformed predictions about an enormous audience and bestseller status, most letters ramble on, trying to do everything at once. Margins get thinner, font sizes smaller, and everything gets lost.

A good submission has a fairly brief, carefully written cover letter and includes:

- An explanation of why you have chosen to submit to this agent or house
- Highlights of the writer's career/education (past high school only)
- A three-sentence description of the book including the genre and—for God's sake—the title
- Author endorsements if you have any
- The word count
- A mention of the audience/market
- A sentence about why you are uniquely qualified to write this book
- All relevant contact information

The list of things we do not need to know is too long to print here, but highlights include:

- Testimony from your mother/father/sibling/friend
- Your promise it will be a bestseller
- Your confidence that it will be a major motion picture starring Tom Cruise
- Assurances of your willingness to go on *Oprah*
- Any self-comparisons to John Grisham, Stephen King, or J. K. Rowling
- The fact that the book is one of ten manuscripts sitting in your desk drawer

Attach, as separate items, a two-page synopsis, a one-page bio or a résumé, and a marketing plan if you want. If it is not something we can use, we can set it aside. If we need more information, we can refer to the collateral material.

The short bio within the cover letter should mention past books (and sales if they were good and maybe even a few words of a good review from a prestigious source), previous publications (no more than three; save the rest for the one-page bio), education, professional credentials (if applicable), honors and awards, and where you live. Do not mention hobbies unless they are directly related to your subject matter, do not mention husbands or wives unless they are famous authors, and do not mention any affiliations having nothing to do with writing. And do not mention your pets. I do not know why people end their bios with sentences like "Jane B. Plain lives in Modesto, California, with her husband, Dick, and her cockatoo, Hemingway, her dog, Faulkner, and her cats, F. Scott and Zelda II." It makes you sound like a lightweight.

The description is tough. Not every book lends itself to a three-line synopsis, sometimes called a "handle" in publishingspeak. Some great books would sound ridiculous if boiled down to thirty careless words: *A man wanders around Ireland's capital bumping into people. The book ends in an 8,000-word sentence with only one piece of punctuation . . .* or *. . . An old Cuban guy, who hangs around a young boy, goes fishing and catches a big fish.* It is not easy, but if enough effort is put in, a writer can hone a couple of sentences to capture the essence and story. Not every character's relationship needs to be addressed, nor every nuance of the plot: *A 13-year-old girl and her younger brother, orphaned by a tornado in rural Oklahoma, are forced to find their own way to California in 1932.* That Ribbon of Highway *chronicles their journey through migrant camps, food riots, and lynch mobs to find their only surviving kin and a new place to call home.* This story could have many additional characters and story lines, but they are not needed for the handle. The description is the most difficult portion of a cover letter because it is the most valuable. It takes a lot of work to make something sound simple. It is worth it because, if it is done right, those words will be the basis for our pitches and even promotional copy.

As for marketing and audience, unless you have some knowledge that we would not know or could not guess, leave it out. If your book is about the Battle of Gettysburg, we already know millions of people are interested in the Civil War. If your book is a novel about an airplane, do not tell us that 115 million people fly every year and they will all buy a copy. But, if your book is about, say, the history of the Corvette and you know that 500,000 people subscribe to *Corvette Magazine* and 300,000 belong to Corvette societies, mention it. Do not, however, make any sales guarantees. We will draw our own conclusions.

Similarly, refrain from comparing your book to known bestsellers. If your novel is about the Civil War, do not mention *Cold Mountain*. If your novel is a legal thriller, do not mention *The Firm*. We know big books; if comparisons are to be made, then we will make them. If your book is similar to a previous title, and a comparison is obvious, mention the similarities and differences: My book *The Corvette Legacy* should be attractive to the same audience that sent the late Dale Driver's *Corvettes: The American Dream* (1986) into eleven printings, but will draw new readers with an update on the last twenty years of innovations and newer models.

Instead of being succinct and understated, which editors and agents find intriguing, many writers play the cover letter fast and loose, which we find annoying. Worse than too much information, however, is the writer who decides to employ misguided creativity, often with sadly hilarious results.

52. You Got Cute and Made a Fool of Yourself

In an effort to stand out or seem special, many writers resort to a variety of cheap theatrics and low-rent special effects. Many authors choose to adorn their submissions with color graphics such as rainbows, angels, and even scantily clad women. I suppose it is only a matter of time before a submission includes a rendering of a scantily clad angel sitting on a rainbow.

We are unimpressed that you own a color printer.

Sometimes the cover letter is printed out to emulate professional stationery with a meant-to-impress title following the writer's name:

JASPER DI CHEESEYSCRIBE III
WRITER EXTRAORDINAIRE, MARKETING CONSULTANT

Or . . .

Anita Spellchecker
Astrologer, World Peace Facilitator, Poet, Novelist

These writers might as well have added Pain in the Ass or Kooky Hack to their signatures.

Another bad choice we see a lot of is creative font usage as well as tired bells and whistles like shadowing letters, bolding, underlining, and all caps. Many writers try to add a bit of class by using fonts normally associated with wedding invitations. Mistake. You cannot go wrong with

12-point Times New Roman or, if you are feeling saucy, Garamond.

Author photos are common and not too irksome. For some reason, many authors over the years have included pictures of themselves with their pets. I have built a little collection on my bulletin board for no logical reason. It is beginning to look like a vet's office.

A consideration killer is always the writer's notion of a cover. I do not know what the cause is, but writers, even good ones, have no design sense. In the hundreds of cases where authors submitted their vision of jacket art, it has always been laughable. Please do not do this. If you are offered a contract, there will be a point where you will be asked about your cover ideas, though usually only as a courtesy. Wait until then to look tasteless.

A more common blunder is the ham-handed opening:

Dear Editor,
Have you ever wondered what life would be like if you were a woodchuck with attention deficit disorder? So have I and millions of others. I explore this in The Woodchuck Who Couldn't Chuck . . .

Or . . .

Dear Agent,
What would you do if you were suddenly thrust into a world of international intrigue when the CIA recruits you as a covert assassin even though you are a grocery clerk in Billings, Montana? If you're like Josh McDiddle in Paper, Plastic, or . . . Death?! *you'd accept the call to arms, cover your shifts, and head off to Libya . . .*

There are so many ways to go wrong with a heavily stylized introduction. Even if the first reader is charmed, the odds are good someone up the ladder is put off. Being direct, honest, and understated is the most risk-free, professional way to go.

I suppose it is the fault of how-to books telling writers to grab the editor's or agent's attention. There are better ways to increase the odds of floating to the top and being taken seriously. Keep it simple. Do not use tricks and gimmicks like colored ink, graphics, florid typefaces, cheesy photos, and hot-pink letterhead. It smacks of amateurism and desperation. An old adage comes to mind, "Don't look hungry. It makes people want to kick you."

---

53. You Made Stupid Mistakes

A lot of submissions might otherwise have been interesting, except the author made sloppy errors, left out vital information, or ignored the rules. In a profession where protocols are valued, writers are judged partially by their ability to follow the directions.

Every house and agency has fairly simple, straightforward, and easily ascertainable submission requirements, such as two chapters and a cover letter, or just a query and a few pages. They exist so we can manage the amount of incoming mail in relation to our time. We like our guidelines and when it is clear that you, at best, did not bother to find out what they were or, at worst, ignored them, we respond accordingly (rejection or slushdom). Every publishing house lists its guidelines in the *Writer's Market* (which you should own) and the *Literary Market Place* (which you should find at the library). Most houses will mail you their guidelines if you send them an SASE and many have them posted on their Web sites.

Many writers fail to include rudimentary information about their book. I cannot tell you how frustrating it can be when a cover letter does not mention the book's genre or the word count. Some lacked the title, as mentioned above, and a couple contained no contact information for the author. I hope they are not waiting for the phone to ring.

Many submissions go out without having undergone a spell check or a basic edit. I have read repeated paragraphs, seen sentences combined with others making no sense or sentences that end abruptly, half-complete. It is obvious advice, but I will say it again: Don't let ur lettur leave your house with a typos in itt. When material comes to us like this, it asks, even demands, to be rejected or ignored.

---

54. You Got Lazy or Impatient

Agents can represent only a finite number of writers. When they send something out, editors judge them by the quality of their submissions. When you ask an agent to sign you, you are asking him to stake his income and reputation on you. When you ask a publishing house to publish you, you are asking for a commitment of at least tens of thousands of dollars and often more. Editors must, like agents, put their careers on the line, to a degree, based on your abilities and assurances.

Why, with the stakes so high, do so many writers feel that learning the name of the person from whom they are asking for a show of faith is an undue burden? Dear Editor and Dear Agent submissions are lazy and unimpressive, especially knowing mail merge functions make it easier than ever to personalize correspondence. (I regularly receive mail addressed to Ms. or Miss Pat Walsh—an honest mistake, but since I am a man, it does not make me bask in self-confidence. I once opened a letter to read, *Dear Ms. Walsh, It was lovely meeting you . . .* Thanks a lot.)

Of course, attention-grabbing submissions have more than just my correctly spelled name on the top. If the writer mentions she has read a book, or some of the books, I have edited and thus feels I will appreciate her work, it means she has done some homework and I am getting a look at something targeted to me, not mass-mailed.

Most books published today have an acknowledgments section in the front or back. Editors and agents are usually listed. If you regularly read in the genre in which you write—which you must—you should be able to narrow the field of agents and editors who might be interested in your work. The agent's or editor's contact information is easy to find in the many trade reference manuals or on publishersmarketplace.com. Targeted cover letters will get more attention and a submission will get a more careful read.

Another useful practice underutilized by writers is to send a sample of your writing to an author you admire. Excepting some best-selling heavyweights, many successful authors are appreciative of their situation and are willing to give advice and, sometimes, referrals. If you get such a referral or endorsement, then feature it prominently in the cover letter.

These things take time as well as energy. So many writers are in a hurry they end up waiting their whole life.

Waiting is every author's second job. You wait for answers, you wait for edits, you wait for covers. You wait for reviews, for promotion plans, for sales figures. If you do not like waiting, get used to it, or find a different line of work.

Publishing is an industry that moves at glacial speed most of the time. We move slowly, considering options, weighing decisions, calculating. Manuscripts sit on desks for months. Then suddenly, we sense competition, buzz, heat, and we burst into action. We suddenly stake our claim to a project, disturb publishers on vacation, set off bidding wars, alert the sales force, and start entertaining bestseller dreams. Sometimes we even work Friday afternoons.

For those moments to happen, you have to wait for them. After talent and dedication, patience is an author's greatest tool. The key is to use the time you have productively and the best way to do that is to work on the next book, revise the one you have, or research new ideas or new markets for your existing titles.

It is fine to follow up on submissions after the response period listed in the agent's or editor's submission guidelines. A light prodding will not hurt, but one of the worst things a writer can do is push for the quick answer. It is never the one you want.

The surest way to get out of the slush pile or spend as little time in it as possible is to show your submission as much sincerity and commitment as you are asking an agent or editor to show your book and your career.

PART SIX

AGENTS PROVOCATEURS

Though most writers know that having an agent is a significant step toward publication, most do not know exactly what an agent does and how the submission process works.

WARNING: If you skipped forward to this chapter hoping to find out the secret to landing an agent, you are going to writer's hell where you will spend eternity proofreading the *Unabomber's Manifesto* while listening to the book-on-tape of *Mein Kampf* read by the author. Either that or spend forever in my office attempting the Sisyphean task of trying to organize my files and picking up all the chewed-up pen caps.

I was going to begin this chapter with a forced attempt at humor by telling an anecdote about how many times I have been asked, *How do I find an agent?*, but the subject is worn out. It is already clear that would-be authors desperately want to find the perfect agent—someone who will fawn over them, praise their names among the literati, return their calls promptly or actually take them, no matter who he has to hang up on. Someone who will squeeze hundreds of thousands of dollars out of publishers and fly across the country to slap the face of any reviewer who dares utter an unkind word about the author's book. My anecdote was going to attempt to illustrate how some writers think there is a surefire, closely guarded process to finding such an agent. Some writers do feel there is some sort of secret to getting ideal representation. In truth, most writers know there is no secret. It is just hard, hard work finding an agent and nothing about it is funny.

Actually, when writers ask *the question,* what they are really asking most times is if I will refer them to someone I know. If I have read their stuff, and it is pretty good, I might. If I have not read anything, or did not like it, I pretend to be horrible at remembering names. This act of chickening out is so the writer does not submit something fetid with my name in the query letter, making the agent question my taste. When I do give a writer an agent's name, it is because I think the connection might work for both of them, although this matchmaking has worked only about 10 percent of the time. A one-in-ten shot is a hell of a lot better of a chance than most writers give themselves when they go after every agent at once. Of the many ways to approach an agent, the wide net is the least productive and the most annoying.

55. You Accidentally Went into the Junk-Mail Business

You may think you are covering all bases by downloading a list of every literary agent and submitting samples to all of them; but what you are really doing is producing a limited run of junk mail.

Any agent who can afford to be choosy is going to be biased against a wide, impersonal submission for good reasons. If the submission is going out to everybody and it is wonderful, chances are it has already been snatched up. If it has not, it probably is not any good. Multiple submissions with generic cover letters are not given priority by any agent. Sending out your book is saying you are worthy of being published and deserving of the best deal out there. So if you are a writer ready for publication, if your work is worthy of a big advance, if what you have to say is important enough for many people to spend their money on, why then would you think it was a good idea to let just anyone be the champion of something so important? The only agent who will take a mass mailing seriously is a spare-room tycoon who has no clients and is at the bottom of the food chain.

56. You Do Not Know What You Are Looking For

When seeking an agent, keep in mind what you are looking for when you ask for literary representation. You want someone who will stake her reputation on your work. Someone who will manage what you hope turns out to be a large portion of your income. Someone empowered to argue for your legal rights and artistic protection. Who oversees the future of your career, stands by you, and stands up for you. I swear to God, you do not want just anyone. You want someone who believes in you and what you are doing and not just hopes that you will make them some dough. You want someone who will drink the Kool-Aid. And you deserve it, if you are truly ready.

When I conceived the idea for this book, which incidentally began as a biography of Ulysses S. Grant and evolved into this how-to book, I was torn about which agent to represent it, or whether or not to even get an agent. I know a lot of agents, and some of them even like me, usually the ones with high tolerance for unreturned phone calls and lost manuscripts. The reason I approached the agent I did was because she pissed me off. I had bought a couple of titles from this agent and had tough but friendly negotiations; I learned to respect and like her. We attended a ball game together and I had her over to my house for a poker game. I liked her so much, I did not even get mad when she won all my money. Months later, I was asked to go back to a number of agents to amend several contracts in order to change a small codicil that was burdening our accounts department. Every agent

I approached was amenable except the agent in question, whom I had expected no trouble from. *No,* she said. *I know it is a small thing, but it is not in my client's best interest and I am not going to bend.* I was mad. After some time had passed, I realized it was not about personalities or favors, it was about fiduciary responsibility and duty. When I needed an agent, I knew immediately whom to turn to. I wish every writer the satisfaction I have had with my agent. There is a point to this story beyond me kissing up to my agent. When considering representation, you want to find someone who will trust you and whom you can trust. Do not sign up with someone just because they are willing to take you on as a client. If you are as good as you think you are, act like it.

---

57. You Did Not Research Agents

The best way to attract the right agent is to act like the right client. Start by being professional and doing some research. Compile a list of authors you enjoy and respect—not just authors whose success you are envious of. In fact, do not start with the agents of iconic authors like Anne Rice and J. K. Rowling. Begin with authors whose writing and communication skills you admire, even if they are little known. Look in the back of their books, usually their earlier titles, and find out who their agent is. Check out the agent's listing in the *Literary Marketplace* at your local library. Go to their Web site. No group besides lovers of pornography has benefited from the advent of the Internet more than writers.

Besides being a wondrous tool for fact checking and research, the Net offers opportunities to find and check the background of agents. Check writers' Web sites like Predators & Editors to see if there is a general consensus about them. Google them. Find other authors who are represented by them and ask them questions to determine if you and the agent would be a good fit. Do this with several agents.

When you are ready, and I mean honestly ready, to send your sample to your carefully selected group of agents, mention in each letter why you have chosen to submit to that particular agent. Demonstrating that you have done your homework ahead of time will almost always increase the amount of attention your submission receives. Give the agent a reasonable time to exclusively look at your work. When you get rejected, or too much time passes, go on to the next agent.

A greater advantage can be gained not only by learning the names of an agent's authors, but by getting their endorsement, thereby transforming your blind pitch into a client referral, the best possible introduction to an agent.

58. You Did Not Go to Published Authors

Many people in publishing will not like my saying this, but I think submitting a short bit of your writing directly to a published author is an effective way to gain access to agents. Clients who refer writers to their agents feel good about nurturing a new talent; if it works out, they have done the agent a favor.

Except for the big names, most authors get less mail than you might expect. I would estimate that an author receives one piece of mail, including fan mail, hate mail, blurb requests, and writing samples, per two thousand copies of his book sold per month. So an author who has sold fifty thousand copies of his book might get twenty-five pieces of mail a month, which is not an overwhelming chore.

A few tips: Just as a matter of course, handwrite the envelope at least. Being professional with an agent or editor is fine, but what you are doing when approaching an author is asking for a personal favor and script is more personal than a laser printer. If you enjoyed the author's work, tell her boldly. But do not be unctuous; writers do not trust unmitigated praise unless it comes in the form of a book review. Do not track down the author's home address on the Internet or by searching through property records. Send your request through the publisher, who generally forwards mail to the author, the exceptions being very famous or controversial authors—in these cases the publisher usually forwards the mail to an agent. Agents are less likely to send mail on because, as the author's representative, they feel comfortable opening the author's correspondence and are likely to cull anything that might distract from her promotional duties or next book.

59. You Submitted Your Work Too Early

The single biggest reason good writers with good books have trouble finding an agent is they submit queries and samples before they are ready. The elation of typing "The End" seems to inspire writers to slap on a cover letter and hit the post office, not wanting to wait another moment to begin their careers. It's the wrong thing to do, and premature submissions can have long-lasting ill effects.

I think it is best for writers to believe they have only one shot with everyone they send their book to—because they do. I cannot speak for all editors, but I am never impressed when a writer calls to check on his submission only to have him mention that it may be a bit rough, or he will fix something in the next draft. Writers who submit something, then send new pages and chapters to replace old ones are wasting their time. It is an automatic pass.

Once you are confident in your manuscript, you need to make sure your collateral material is in top shape, too.

60. Your Query Is Queer

A good query letter is simple, elegant, and intriguing. It is also harder to write than a symphony in C minor for the tuba. Faced with the daunting task of defining your work and self on one page, too many writers choose to go lazy or crazy, as I wrote in the last chapter. Lazy comes when the author slaps together a couple of paragraphs without even spell checking. Crazy comes when she decides to impress the agent with a bunch of gimmicky constructions and inane literary embroidery. Both methods make it easy for the agent to send the submission back promptly.

Sadly, good manuscripts often are saddled with lousy cover letters and collateral materials. Why someone who has spent ten years writing a book would top it off with a boring or absurd letter is beyond me. The cover letter and, indeed, any correspondence representing a writer should be given a great deal of care.

---

61. You Cannot Stop Talking About Yourself

I have seen writers' biographies so long I thought they were the manuscript. The short bio should be easy, but it is often bloated and unfocused. It is not an outline for your autobiography; it is a specific listing of salient details pertaining to your book and your relevant experience. Again, the simpler the better. Three simple declarative sentences stating where you were born, where you graduated from your highest level of education, and some highlights of your writing career. Do not discuss your motivation for writing, do not mention the name of the high school English teacher who inspired you, and as I have said before, do not mention your pets.

62. You Cannot Describe Your Own Work

A good synopsis requires many drafts and, if you have a trusted reader, another set of eyes to ensure that you are not too close to your book to boil it down accurately. Otherwise, there are no hard-and-fast rules. If your novel is plot-driven, start with your main characters and describe their situation with a hint toward the ending. If your book is a business advice book, jump to the benefits a reader might get. If your book is a collection of Turkish limericks, good luck to you, you are on your own. When you finally distill the essence of your book into a few lines, you will know it. If you have done it right, it will be a real boost to your chances of publication.

I have counseled against the use of loved ones as manuscript readers, but family and friends can be invaluable in one area: the synopsis. Recently, I attended a writers' conference in the Pacific Northwest where I met with several dozen writers. Every time I asked someone to submit a sample of their work, they asked me if I would also like a synopsis as well. "No thanks," I said. Every single would-be author expressed relief. "Unless you think your synopsis is really, really good," and I mostly received sheepish looks. Writers are hopelessly bad at synopsizing their own work. Another person, interested but not entrenched in the book, can be a helpful sounding board for how an entire book is condensed into a few lines.

Remember, the longer your synopsis, the less likely the agent will read the actual submission.

63. You Lied

Do not lie to agents. Not even a little bit.

Do not embellish your biographical material in your query letter. Do not say your work has been published in *The New York Times* if they printed your letter to the editor or your classified ad. Do not say your work was nominated for the Pulitzer Prize if you sent it in with the fifty-dollar fee yourself.

Do not list phony degrees or publishing credits. Or make up bogus awards. Or include blurbs from dead authors.

Getting ahead is rough, but it is not worth being a scumbag. Telling the truth is a writer's job; and if you start by betraying that, you will be reviled when you are discovered.

64. You Do Not Understand the Agent/Author Relationship

Your agent is your voice when it comes to the business side of publishing. Lately, as editors get more bogged down in business and promotion, agents have become first readers and often work with editors to polish material, especially on second books. When you have an agent, it is important to know what he is supposed to do, what he is not obligated to do, and what he is not supposed to do. All of the following come from my actual experience with agents.

An agent should approach publishers and secure an offer, then negotiate the deal to the best terms he can and not accept an offer without the author's approval. He is in charge of enforcing the contract and watching the money flow. He is supposed to argue on your behalf when there is a contract dispute.

The agent is not obligated, though he is entitled, to mediate noncontract issues the author is reluctant or unable to handle herself, such as promotional opportunities, questions of production and deadlines, and the author's dissatisfaction with general marketing.

The agent is not supposed to start problems by second-guessing the editorial direction of a book if the author does not feel it is a problem. He is not supposed to borrow money from the author's royalty account. He is not supposed to interfere in subsidiary rights that he does not control.

65. You Sullied Your Name

I have overheard many conversations between agents where they joke about the awful submissions they have received and they have no trepidation about sharing the name of a writer who has perversely amused them. If there is anything agents are good at, it is remembering names. When you make an ass of yourself with one agent, there is a good chance it will get around. This is particularly true at writers' conferences, by the way.

---

66. You Scare Away Agents

Finding an agent is not unlike finding a mate. You have to accentuate your positives to show confidence but not build yourself up too much lest you seem egomaniacal. Be charming and be funny if you can while still appearing serious. Be honest and sincere. Or, at least appear to be so.

Do not be creepy. Do not call at odd hours or display some sort of obsessive-compulsive overcommunication. If they want more information, they know how to use a phone.

What if you are generally a little neurotic or quirky? Fine. Agents expect it from writers. But, if you lead with your more high-maintenance side, they will assume you will really become a wacko when they get to know you.

At the risk of beating the dating anthology to death, let familiarity come slowly and allow the relationship to grow over time. Never sleep with your agent, unless it is in your contract. I think I just killed the analogy.

67. The Dark Side of Agents

It is sad that writers have to race around begging for an agent to take a chance on them rather than the other way around. Actually, it is not sad, it is sick. The agent works for the author, not the converse. The agent should worry about not being able to reach the author; but it is a buyer's market for representatives and the situation is unlikely to change anytime soon. Every now and again, someone will print out some cheap stationery and call herself a literary agent so she can represent her own book. Who would be fooled by that? It never works.

Anyone who sets up a Web page and produces a shoddy business card can call themselves a literary agent—drawing a bunch of clients to choose from in short order. Some writers are hungry enough to sign on without asking any questions like, *How long have you been in business?* and *What experience do you have?* A good rule might be to not let anyone manage your career who you would not trust to water your houseplants. Recently, a woman who had proclaimed herself a literary agent charged a passel of writers a load of money and faked her death before fleeing to Europe.

One of my biggest gripes with agents, particularly large corporate agencies, is the emphasis they put on self-advocacy rather than on the client. I have heard some really untoward bullshit from time to time. When a contract is negotiated, some bigshots worry about something in the contract reflecting on their image rather than what is in the client's best interest. One agent told me he would not even entertain our offer if the contract contained certain items, insisting he did not consider the offer legitimate unless it conformed to the agency's in-house parameters—designed to enhance the agency, not its clientele. One agent tried to include an agency clause—a standard agreement between the author and the agent governing their financial relationship that, for some reason, is included in the publisher's contract with the author—giving the agent a percentage of whatever the author earned from writing in the future. Fortunately, these instances are rare.

68. The Agent Rejection

Many agents are former editors who got sick of publishing's long hours and low pay or got squeezed out during one of the many mergers. Some agents are lawyers who like advocating for artists rather than criminals or corporate CEOs or combinations thereof. And every legitimate agent I have met loves books and is always looking for talented authors.

Agents often reject writers with the *I'm not taking on any new clients right now* or *My list is full* shtick, but it is a brush-off. It does not mean your book is bad, although it could. A gentle no usually means your book is not exciting enough to make room for it at the time or it needs more work than an agent can give it.

If you are having no luck landing an agent, then you need to explore the reasons why. Sure, it's tough, but it's not impossible. If you find yourself following protocol and exploiting opportunities and are still unsuccessful, you need to make some hard choices. You can try to improve your book, write a new one, or give up.

Nothing in this field comes easy except heartbreak and disappointment. The work it takes to get an agent is no exception, but it will scare off the timid and repel the slothful, leaving you an edge. If you go above and beyond, you will distinguish yourself from a large percentage of writers out there and, at the very least, be read and considered seriously.

PART SEVEN

ACQUIRING MINDS

Knowing what editors' concerns and needs are will help every writer approach the writing, packaging, and submission of a book to help avoid costly mistakes.

69. You Don't Know What Editors Do

There are two types of editors: those who go to meetings more than they talk on the phone and those who talk on the phone more than they go to meetings. I like to think of myself as the rare combination of both. The only time I get off the phone is if I have to go to a meeting and the only reason a meeting breaks up is because everyone has calls to make. When do we edit books? On the train or bus. The manifestation of anyone's editorial skill is directly proportional to the length of one's commute. No editor worth his salt drives to work.

Though editors do edit books, some of them extensively, there are much more prosaic duties that fill their days. The increasingly prevalent aspect of the job is chaperoning the book through the entire publishing cycle, both within the house and in the stores. We are the author's advocate to garner marketing dollars and promotion attention. We pitch the books to our own salespeople in hopes of passing on our enthusiasm. Most important, we are the primary contact when a problem arises in any area regarding the book. The editor is the only one who cannot say, "That's not my problem," when the inevitable screw-up happens.

But the most important job an editor has is finding new books. Today's editors are not just looking for a good book, they're searching for a book with a good story and I'm not talking about the plot.

We want a book with a back story that generates excitement. A book with a blurb attached from a literary icon, a second novel that took an author thirty years to write after her first was well received. Or a fascinating author history, like Christy Nolan, an Irish paraplegic who wrote a great book by blinking to his mother in code. Or the rare instance of someone finding a new way to tell a story that's been told many times before. When a manuscript comes along with a premise that instantly fascinates or elicits a reaction like *What a great idea for a book,* it gets editors abuzz.

Maybe because it's so hard most of the time, when a book comes along that seems like it might just sail over the marketplace obstacles, it makes us giddy.

These books, however, are few and far between. A great deal of an editor's time—outside of meetings—is spent developing or maintaining relationships with agents and other sources of new books. To be successful, editors must be in on a number of agents' submission lists. We will not last long watching other editors buy hot books while we read about it in *Publishers Weekly*. If an editor reads a book and decides to pass, and it later sells for a lot of money, that's bad for him. If he never saw it at all, that's really bad. Being among the first to see new material is a vital part of the editing job. It means that you are relevant and respected. What relationships you have and how you rate against your peers is the second most worrisome aspect of being an editor. The first is sales.

How an editor's book sells is the final number. You do not get judged on how the book reviewed, or how smoothly it went through production, or how happy the author is. It has to sell.

This is a business. You take a chance, you get a return. The problem with publishing is that the bigger the chance you take, the return is the same. If an editor buys a first novel aimed at the prime demographic (women between twenty-five and forty-five years old) from a well-published young writer with an M.F.A. and a stack of published short stories for a ten-thousand-dollar advance and it sells a respectable ten thousand copies (pronounced "fifteen thousand" to everyone outside the publishing house), the editor is on solid ground. If she does the same thing with a tougher book, say an edgy story aimed at a different audience, say men between eighteen and thirty, and sells the same number of copies, she is still credited with only ten thousand units by the number crunchers upstairs, despite the fact that the title was exponentially harder to sell because the audience is more fickle (lazy) and harder (more expensive) to reach.

Jeesh, this is depressing. Perhaps it's not too late to try for a career in something easier like particle physics, less demanding like classical ballet, or with a brighter future like haberdashery.

---

70. You Do Not Know What Most Writers Do Not Know

What many writers today do not realize is that they can, if they do the work, go straight to an editor, even at a big New York house. It's just a bit harder. Like researching agents, the acknowledgment page of a book is a great source of names. If you think you've found the right name within, by all means, submit directly. Just be careful to give him enough room to do his work before tracking him down. If he likes it, but cannot publish it for whatever reason (there are many), he may be willing to refer you to an agent. If he does like your work and wants to make an offer, you'll be amazed how easy it is to get an agent.

PART EIGHT

BAD MOJO

There are reasons you cannot control, but that doesn't mean you're licked.

71. You Have Bad Luck and Bad Timing

Here's the real bad news. You could do everything right—write a very good book, land a big-shot agent—and still not get published. Or you could get published and not sell, effectively ending your career. It happens a lot. Every agent I know has clients they could not or cannot sell. Some agents hang on until publishing tides turn—new editors get hired, new imprints form, and so on—or they let the client go.

Ready for some more bad news? If you do absolutely everything right and you still remain unpublished, then I do not know what to tell you except, "Damn. Can I buy you a beer?" There is just no mitigating bad luck. But luck comes in streaks and if there is something that mitigates bad luck, it's time. Time and patience favor the committed and the talented and for most, I believe, things work out. But not in every instance, just so you know. I'm sorry to waffle, but there are no promises.

Hard-luck stories are as common in the writing game as misplaced modifiers. Every writer has a few. I talked to one woman who had her book under contract twice only to have both publishing houses fold shortly before her pub date. (I passed on that book fast.) I hear from writers who sign with an agent only to have him die right after. Or their editors were fired before the contract could be signed. It's tough. The only way to make bad luck worse is to accept it, making it a permanent disability rather than a temporary condition.

72. You Accept Bad Luck and Bad Timing

John Kennedy Toole was a dedicated writer who could not, literally, for the life of him find a publisher. He gave up on publishing the hard way, by committing suicide. His mother shopped his manuscript around for ten years before finding a publisher, a small university press in Louisiana. *A Confederacy of Dunces* won the Pulitzer Prize in 1980.

The lesson here, of course, is hire your mother as your agent. Actually, the Toole story teaches us that perseverance pays off and timing is everything. If he'd been able to find a publisher in the early seventies, I do not think the world would have been quite ready for his work, and he might have been ignored and forgotten. Then again, I do not think Mrs. Toole would have let that happen.

The timing of a book is everything. A book can be the spark that lights the world afire, but the underlying conditions have to be there. *On the Road* by Jack Kerouac had the youthful dissatisfaction that lay dormant under the doldrums of the 1950s as a launching point just as *In Cold Blood* fulfilled people's need to know the gory details of society's underbelly during the same time. Erica Jong's *Fear of Flying* spoke to underlying personal and cultural desires of women, and *To Kill a Mockingbird* appealed to the American sensibilities of justice and individuality that badly needed shoring up.

The above authors, as groundbreaking writers almost always are, were probably told the timing was wrong for their books but they persevered. If you know your book is needed now, trust that. If you suspect that your book is not ready to find an audience, trust that and put it away until it sits right with you. Again, the great advantage held by first-time writers is that they control their own pace without pressure from editors and agents.

73. You Are Caught in a Topical Storm

One of the most blatant disservices writers do to their careers is chase headlines and hot topics. They see books coming out in a genre or about a particular subject and they try to ride the wave. The problem is that it's always too late. On September 18, 2001, I received my first query for a novel about the events of 9/11. A few months later, full manuscripts with the tragedy as a central or supporting theme started arriving. More recently, I've seen dozens of manuscripts about the unseemly side of priest/altar boy relationships—most of them a little more colorful than I can stomach.

This mistake will waste more of your time and energy than any other. If you pick the issue of the day and crank out the book in six months, then get an agent and a publisher in sixty days, you're still a year away from hitting the shelves. You best hope your issue has not faded away or some other writer has not beaten you to the marketplace. There are many tens of thousands of issue-driven books in desk drawers out there.

Writers have some degree of duty to reflect in a meaningful way on matters of import. But more often than not, they try to capitalize on hot-button issues not realizing that the span of time from the moment they start writing until they get published under the most expeditious circumstances is eighteen months. The wide audience they had hoped to impress has moved on. To capitalize on a news issue, you have to have been just published, and your book has to have serious relevance to the topic. You cannot plan for it unless you have some inside knowledge. Besides, if you write a topical novel or narrative nonfiction work, you run the risk of your book becoming stale and going out of print quickly.

There are, of course, exceptions to this rule where a piece of writing actually becomes a societal fulcrum; but for every *Uncle Tom's Cabin* there are ten thousand manuscripts that rot in file cabinets becoming more irrelevant with every passing day. Just write your book to the utmost of your abilities including the thematic points you find important and relevant. But beware of choosing such a theme based on what you think will make the book more marketable rather than what you really believe.

If your title's subject matter seems out of the spotlight, it just gives you more time to improve it so you can be in front of the wave when it comes back. Besides, isn't it better to start trends than follow them?

74. You Blame the Publishing Industry for Your Lack of Success

I'm sorry. I am sorry those of us in the industry are flighty in terms of what we want. I'm sorry our opinions conflict. I'm sorry our protocols are cumbersome. I'm sorry our decisions are unfair. I'm sorry that we're often slow to recognize talent. I'm sorry that we're sometimes full of bull-shit.

And I'm sorry that none of these things is going to change anytime soon, and if it does change, it will probably be for the worse. But we're doing something right. In fact, I would make the case that American literature today is of a higher caliber than at any time in the past hundred years. And the only reason I'm qualifying the time and nation is that I do not know enough about the good and bad writing of other countries or time frames to comment. Today, there's a greater selection of work from a wider range of authors. Even the bad stuff today is better than the bad stuff of yes-teryear. Nobody believes me about this, but go to a used-book store and find an old book you've never heard of by an author you've never heard of and read it. Then go to a new-book store and find a new book in the same genre by a midlist author and compare the two.

I understand that the above begs the question "Why are so many lousy books published?" I'd be a liar if I denied that cruddy books do not find their way on to bookstore shelves, but most published books, and I mean by legiti-mate presses, are not bad for their respective audiences. I might think *The Countess and the Shirtless Blacksmith* (Har-lequin Romance), *Mary-Kate and Ashley: Lost in Des Moines* (Scholastic Books), and *The Turner Diaries* (Crazynutjob Press) are literary treats, and you might (I hope) disagree. But for their audiences, they're just right.

Some writers who have been at the gates too long and racked up an impressive rejection slip collection have a very different view of publishing than mine. They counterattack rejection by bashing the publishing industry from the outside.

They are proud of their work and secretly, and sometimes not so secretly, think it is better than most, if not all, of their contemporaries'. They do not think, upon getting a rejection slip, *Perhaps my book isn't good enough yet. Maybe I should work on it some more.* They think, *What do those friggin' candy-asses know. My book's better than most of that junk out there.*

To them, gone are the gentle ways of the past when editors and publishers cared about literary integrity. They think a rite of passage for an editor today is to trek out to Maxwell Perkins's grave and take a leak. Publishing today cares only about the bottom line, about how much overpriced, overhyped crap they can shove down the throat of a public that doesn't know any better. The publishing strategy today, they feel, is to produce garbage and not let anything great get published because it would upset the status quo and possibly lead to a consumer revolution, endangering the profitability of the pap.

Slightly less paranoid writers blame incompetence rather than the diabolical. The focus on the bottom line has permanently distracted from the ability to recognize the wonderful and the meaningful. "Those jerks wouldn't know a great book if it was left on their doorstep," the bitter writer cries. "I know it for a fact, because that's where I left mine."

Ambition and dedication are not synonymous; they can even be diametrically opposed. Ambition is about you; dedication is about what you're doing. If your goal is to be a famous, rich, powerful author, I have no advice for you. I don't really know anything about how to achieve that (perhaps Tony Robbins has some materials for you). If your goal however is to have a widely read, influential book that has a real effect on readers—be it providing a little escape or changing their lives—then focus on your writing and storytelling and leave the pipe dreams to others.

Holding strong views and being self-confident is fine, but letting bitterness and anger paralyze you will kill your career before it starts. The reason your book is not published may very well be because of flaws in industry practices and priorities. But it does not matter. Publishing is what it is and if you want to be a part of it, you have to accept its failings as well as its attributes.

---

75. You Do Not Take Advantage of Opportunity

Sending out your book or portions of it too early is a mistake, but it's better than letting a good chance pass you by. Exceptional opportunities are just that—exceptions. When you're lucky enough to catch a break like an agent you met at an airport who wants to read your stuff or Salman Rushdie starts dating your daughter, do not sit on your hands paralyzed by fear or laziness. Do something. There are a finite number of instances where you'll have an edge and you never know when they'll come up or how long they will last. A window may open for a day, a week, or a year.

A woman called me once to check in on her submission and in the course of conversation she told me the Pulitzer Prize–winning author Stephen Ambrose had read a chapter and offered to endorse it when it was finished. Have you sent it to him yet? I asked. Nope, she said. I'm waiting until it's been edited, typeset, and proofread, so it's perfect. Of course, Mr. Ambrose passed away shortly thereafter and the woman never got her blurb.

In other words, imperfect action is better than perfect inaction.

---

76. You Are Sticking to Your Guns

The evil twin of dedication is stubbornness. With bulletin boards for writers, writers' personal Web sites, writers' conferences, and especially writing workshops, there are many opportunities for a writer to volunteer his work as a literary piñata for others to take whacks at. And eventually, the author can retreat into a defensive shell where nothing, at least nothing he admits, gets through. Then there are the batches of encouraging rejection slips that tell the writer the book is almost there, if only you'd change everything. After months or years of enduring conflicting advice, phony enthusiasm, and cold rejection, the writer has become entrenched in the idea that the only one who can be trusted with his book is himself. So when he gets real direction, he dismisses it, throwing the baby out with the bathwater.

It's hard to blame these writers, but I still do. Knowing what is right for their book is the writer's job. I think a strong trait many successful writers share is an openness to others' opinions and a good mental filter to discern which bits of advice to hear and then apply to their work and which ones to listen to and then blow off. As a general rule, the best advice is the hardest to listen to.

---

77. You Do Not Go On to the Next Book

The toughest advice to hear is to abandon the book and start a new one. It's tough to tell someone, "It's not right for us, but I'd love to see something else in the future." This is the universal publishing language for "You have some talent, but please drop this book in the recycle bin so it won't be a total waste."

A few years ago, MacAdam/Cage had an entire season of first-time authors. It wasn't planned that way, but it worked out wonderfully. The titles were an eclectic mix—coming of age, historical, quirky, lyrical, edgy—and they were aimed at a variety of audiences—men, women, young, old. The authors, too, were a varied bunch from different parts of the country with different education levels and personal experiences. After getting to know them all, I realized that besides being published for the first time, they had only one thing in common: They all had at least two previous novels in a drawer. Not one of them was debuting with the first, or even second, novel they had written. You could call it coincidence, but it's not.

If you feel your first or latest book is the best it can be and you are not getting a positive response despite diligence, stick it in the closet next to the Christmas ornaments and move on to your next book. The sooner the better. Moving on is one of the hardest, most productive, and necessary acts a writer can commit.

78. You Do Not Take Positive Action

Positive action, an admittedly weak phrasing that would probably sound better in French, is simply moving forward without getting distracted or frustrated.

What constitutes positive action is different for each writer, and, deep down, everyone knows what her version of it is. And not many positive actions are easy, like researching agent names or revising a manuscript for typos or repeated words. Some actions are kind of humbling, like writing a letter to an author for an endorsement. And a few may even feel humiliating, like buying a book listing writers' mistakes.

But everything a writer does should be a best effort to take her closer to her goal and should be as deliberate and thoughtful as she can make it, from doing her research to rewriting her book, from writing a query letter to making a nagging phone call. The option is to remain an also-ran with a lot of time and talent wasted. There is no greater waste of time than giving up.

Too many writers have found contentment in being unpublished or underpublished, a word I just invented that means to be content to get a story posted on a Web site or printed in the weekly circular their brother-in-law edits. They have ceded that getting published is too tough or they are not good enough, connected enough, or lucky enough to get a book published. They've settled for wallowing in self-defeat and surrendered to the misconception that new voices will not be accepted. There are a lot of these people and the funny thing is that a lot of them are good writers who just aren't interested in the rat race of the writing community and agent hunting. They're turned off by self-promotion. They're terrified of rejection.

And these writers are very unlikely to be reading a book like this. But they should, because many of them might make it if they toughen up, buckle down, and move ahead. Because not all the news is bad.

PART NINE

THE GOOD NEWS

14 Reasons Why Your Book Just Might Get Published

1. You Wrote a Good Book

Nothing will further your attempts to be published like having a good book. And when I say good book, I mean a very good book, the best you can write. Of course, everyone who submits a book thinks it's good and deserving of publication, critical accolades, and brisk sales. But, clearly, that's true only a very small percentage of the time. Books that achieve these three successes may have little in common. But a few elements do thread through most successful efforts, whether they be novels or business texts. How do you know if your book is good?

To be sure, answer the following:

- Is your writing deliberate? Is every section, chapter, paragraph, sentence, and word where it's supposed to be and doing the job you mean it to do? If not, should it be moved, or reshaped, or cut? It may be my background in newspapering, but I believe the best way to tell a story is the shortest way possible. (I say this knowing I'm inviting charges of my own exposition, but I say there's a difference between ranting and rambling, the former having value, if only to myself.)

- As a test, open your manuscript to any random page and read a few paragraphs to yourself. Does it have informational value? Is the writing, particularly the verb, sharp? Is the dialogue solid? Does one paragraph compel you to read the next? Too often, writers put a lot of work into chapter beginnings, especially Chapter 1. But they ease up on the body of the work. I've read a lot of spicy openings that lead into bland mush.

• Another test is to imagine that an editor or agent will read just one paragraph of your book to judge your writing talent. Again, open the manuscript at random and pick a graph. Is it strong enough to be a representation of all your talent?

• Is the way you've chosen to structure your work the best method of delivering the text to a reader? Having a complete manuscript is a wonderful feeling, one that can turn to debilitating disgust if you suddenly realize the whole structure is wrong and you need to rewrite. I've seen it happen many times. Authors will realize that the wrong character is the protagonist, or the entire book is told in the wrong tense, or the entire narrative construction is flawed. And they're forced to rewrite or even start over. But I think almost all of them will agree it's worth it.

• Can your book survive deconstruction? If you break your finished book down into its parts, does it still work? Many writers outline before writing a book, but too few keep up the outline during the writing or after they've written a draft. They lose the value that an outline provides in seeing the book's entirety and breadth. It's too easy to lose track of the manuscript's structure after it's written and not see the weak points. Many first efforts are unbalanced, with an overload of information early and rushed scenes late. A freshly written outline will highlight defects to a writer who might otherwise be too close to the work to see its flaws.

- Is this the best possible book you can write? Is there nothing left you can think of, no part that you feel is incomplete or confusing or lacking in any manner? Is the manuscript a better end product than when you imagined it before you started writing? As a writer, you're reaching for every chapter, every sentence, every word to be the best you can do. A writer's worth is measured by his worst demons and best attributes. If the most self-critical parts of his psyche are satisfied with his work, then he's ready to submit as a serious threat.

---

2. You Are Honest with Yourself

In good writing, being honest with the reader is an imperative. Writing establishes authenticity when the author plumbs her emotional well for her characters in her narration, even if it's in third-person omnipotent. Readers appreciate writing that has personality and voice that seems like it was written by a fellow human. Besides, people can be lied to plenty for free ("Your call is very important to us, please continue to hold"). But before a writer can achieve honesty *in* her writing, she must first be honest *about* her writing.

If you can look at your work with dispassion and see where it is lacking, you will be reassured of your abilities to rebuild and rewrite where needed. You're able to discern good ideas hobbled by bad writing and clever language masking shoddy, extraneous thoughts. A committed writer is always looking for constructive—often negative—feedback instead of empty praise. If she can give good feedback to herself, as the one person who truly knows what the work is trying to accomplish, all the better.

A critical eye does not just look for what's wrong. A good part of writing is recognizing the achievements, small and large, that give a work value and protecting them from self-doubt's brutal scythe.

Honesty in writing does not stop on the page. A writer's self-honesty will manifest itself in his dealings with others on the road to publication, including agents, editors, and other writers. It will allow him to be confident.

Honesty is the keel, stopping you from listing too much toward thinking you're as worthless as the devil's idiot sister or the greatest thing to happen to literature since Flaubert flunked out of cooking school. Honesty is a writer's compass, guiding him through the seas of insecurity and past the cliffs of sinful pride.

---

3. You Do Your Homework

In writing a book, finding an agent, and landing a book deal, preparation is the key. Most writers know what they want, but many do not know, or care enough to know, what they need to do to get what they want. They want to skip over the middle steps and move from sitting at the desk with a fetching idea in their heads to the National Book Award ceremony. The serious writer will do the gritty work ahead of time, ensuring a more productive experience. Doing the tough stuff—which is often the most tedious—is what will separate you from the pack. Everything you do in order to get published is a considered act with as little dependence on good luck as possible, from the carefully written cover letter to the specific list of recipients. The prep will change for every writer on every book, but it often includes:

In composing:

- You're writing in a genre you read regularly, even if it's practical nonfiction.
- You have some written idea—an outline, chapter-by-chapter guide, or long synopsis—of what you want the book to accomplish.
- You know what you're writing about before you start writing. Concurrent writing and researching comes across as awkward.
- You own or have easy access to reference materials including a dictionary and thesaurus.
- If your subject is complex, you've done a timeline or organizational chart so you do not get confused.
- You have Wite-Out, or your delete key is working. (A few manuscripts have made me wonder.)

In submitting:

- You research the people you've chosen to submit to. A blanket submission is a last resort.

- Your materials are unimpeachable in their form and technical aspects.
- You've read the submission guidelines for every organization and followed them.
- You research the agents and editors to ensure that they're legitimate.
- You put stamps on the envelopes. (You'd be surprised.)

---

4. You Make Yourself Stand Out

The term "over the transom" comes from writers tossing their pieces through the tilted open ventilation windows above the doors of editors in hopes of being accepted for publication. For all I know, that may have worked in the beginning, but now there are so many people trying to get in the back door and side windows, some days it's like *Night of the Living Dead*. I've had writers call me at home, though I'm not listed. I've found a manuscript on my doorstep from someone who did a property record search to get my address. These stunts did not endear the writer to me; in fact, they made me consider temporary restraining orders.

There are many ways to stand out for the wrong reasons, but when you stand out for the right ones, you increase your odds of publishing your books. I've covered much of this earlier, but it bears repeating:

- Do it on the page. Let your writing be the thing that differentiates your submission from the scads of others.

- Take real care when writing your cover letter, query, and synopsis. Consider these items as part of the book, needing as much attention as your opening paragraph.
- Keep your kooky marketing ideas to yourself.
- Less is more. Give only the highlights of your bio. Let your description be an intriguing tease for your work, not an all-encompassing outline.
- The day of the oddball hook is past. Straightforward language will be refreshing—and respected.
- When following up, be demure within the stated submission review period, firm but polite after the expiration of the reading period.

5. You Have High Hopes and Reasonable Expectations

High hopes are very different from high expectations. Hopes are soft and expectations are hard. Dashed hopes disappoint; shattered expectations scar. Everyone who writes a book has a few outlandish daydreams about tearing up the lists and influencing a generation. Even the guy who wrote *Mac OS X: A User's Guide* gave a passing thought to *what if . . .*

But do not let those hopes congeal into high expectations where every smaller success is a failure.

It can be a fine line. You want to throw your heart into your work and have it be a meaningful measure of you and your talents, but if you go overboard, you will not be able to have the objectivity you need to treat it professionally when there are setbacks. A writer with her expectations out of whack cannot see the benefit of encouraging feedback because to her it's just a slap in the face. Even if she's published, she will not let herself enjoy it much because the expectations game will haunt her with visions of grander and grander success.

The person with high hopes and reasonable expectations, however, will revel in every step he takes forward and will have a healthy outlook on his writing and his potential for publication.

6. You Have a Healthy Perspective

A healthy perspective is as important to a professional writer as the ability to type. Perspective is the lens through which she can see the most productive path forward, through problems, and around stumbling blocks.

A good perspective helps a writer to work productively, too, allowing him to accept possible weaknesses without being frustrated or perhaps even dissuaded from writing at all. Perspective can allow a writer to flow past the quagmire of negative responses, lack of recognition, and see the publishing world for what it is—an imperfect business fraught with contradictions and injustices but possessing good intentions. Perspective staves off bitterness and anger and feeds constructive action.

It's my duty to call authors when a bad review comes in. This is the worst part of an editor's job. Publishing is a subjective business, and every book, no matter how well received by most, will get a bad review. I usually put it off as long as possible to see if some good news comes on the heels of the drubbing so I can mitigate the sting. On one particular occasion, no good news was to be had and the review had hit the Internet. And if there's one thing I can count on, it's authors Googling their own names every half hour. So I made the call. I did not preface it with any words of dilution, because I've found that only makes the experience worse. I just read the review, which went something like this:

> *The debut novel by {author's name} is an impressive collection of clichéd phrasing, misplaced modifiers, and dangling prepositions. The characters are flat, the pacing dull, and the plot absurd . . .*

And it went on and on. I don't think the reviewer even liked the way the author spelled his name. After I finished reading, the author drew a breath and said, "Impressive? All right!" Somehow he found a shortcut through all the nasty emotions like anger and shame, and went straight to being able to laugh at the whole thing. His subsequent reviews were mostly positive, some more than others, but I never worried about him letting the bad reviews depress him or the good reviews overinflate his ego.

7. You Take Advantage of Time

More people who might otherwise be published aren't because they're in too much of a hurry. They submit too early because they just cannot stand to wait any longer. They give in to enthusiasm and angst at the expense of considerate care. Time is the writer's friend although most wouldn't agree. If completely finishing a book takes an extra month or year or five, then it does. If you're not a fast writer, good for you. If your rewrites take forever, then they do. No single thing gets me more excited about reading a manuscript than being told it took the writer ten years to finish the book.

Great writing takes time, and I want to think writers know that, too. Few things annoy me more than the voice mails I get every week from would-be authors asking to re-submit new versions of submissions they sent in a couple of weeks ago. I do not have any confidence that these writers are taking themselves or their work seriously.

Waiting is as much a part of writing and publishing as schmoozing and bullshit. It's what you do with the waiting that counts. Is waiting something you endure, or use? A serious writer will know that waiting is part of her job, and she will use that time to improve her craft by starting a new project, refreshing an old one, or just reading.

Anxiety and impatience are powerful forces and, if put to good use, they can be constructive ones. The many periods of waiting will be less aggravating and more constructive if time is seen as a benefit, not a constraint.

The importance of time management does not end with getting your first book published. Say a publishing house sees some talent and rolls the dice by publishing a flawed work. When this happens, the writer is usually still screwed because the book critics (the little dears!) are likely to exploit the book's flaws and make snippy comments about weak spots. The sales will probably not skyrocket, and the publishing house (and other publishing houses) will be disinclined to double-down again with the author. There are few hurdles higher on a writer's career track than trying to get over poor sales and bad or even tepid reviews of a first book.

If the first book is received well, however, another problem presents itself: the sophomore slump. First novels are special and reviewers go a bit easy on them. Booksellers like to lay claim to discovering a new voice and can be convinced to take a chance and order several copies. Barnes & Noble and Borders both have a wonderful program designed to find exciting new authors. Many readers, although not as many as we'd like, also enjoy finding something new.

But a second book has a past. After the first book has had some time in the marketplace, there's a trail of numbers following it outlining sales and return rates—the percentage of books that were shipped out into the world and the number that were sent back to the publisher unsold. There are reviews—good and bad—on file. Unless the first book really achieved success, the second book will be judged almost solely on the performance of its predecessor and the followup's future will be viewed as a rote exercise in publishing math.

One might think that you can predict the commercial life of a second book by taking the number of sales of the first book—because everyone who bought the first book will buy the author's next title—and double it to account for the number of readers who'll come into the fold from a similar marketing effort. Add the few strays who bought the book used or checked it out from the public library and who do not want to wait to get it on the cheap the second time and you've got a nice audience.

But it does not work that way. In most instances, second books do not sell as well as first books, though they should.

Why? Because generally they're not as good. A writer's second book is more important than his first. He has a lifetime to write the first one but he'll be pressured, if his debut was a success, to finish his second in as little as a year. He must resist this pressure and take as much time as he needs to perfect his book, just as he did the first.

Taking the time to properly construct your second book has the added benefit of allowing your first book to further saturate the readership by being recommended through word of mouth. So why do publishers and agents push the author to turn in a second book prematurely? Self-interest and greed, of course. There's a high turnover rate in the publishing field and agents want to sell a second book to the same editor who bought the first before she jumps ship to another house or, God forbid, becomes an agent herself with ideas of poaching authors on her mind. Editors want an easy acquisition and a safe-bet title. Having a publishing track record makes filling in the profit-and-loss form fairly simple. Besides, no one likes waiting.

8.   You Are Patient but Persistent

If you want to be an author, you have to get used to fine lines and subtle distinctions, not the least of which is the difference between being a conscientious writer and a stalker. When your work is ready to submit and you've chosen some agents or editors to approach, you're going to feel some anticipation and even a little giddiness. But a week or so after the envelopes have gone out, those feelings are probably going to ferment into dread and doubt. Did the agent/editor read it yet? Do they even know it's there? Did they hate it? Did they even get it? The idea to kill two birds with one stone will develop: Why not e-mail and confirm delivery? Harmless enough. But after a few days, the e-mail is unreturned, buried, you rightly assume, under a ton of spam. Perhaps sending a short note? Days pass. The urge to pick up the phone develops. Calling under the auspices of innocuous diligence might yield some indication of their opinion or be a gentle nudge to read the submission sooner. So you call and leave a voice mail. Then another . . .

Meanwhile, your worst-case scenario is developing in a conference room somewhere. A meeting is taking place where someone brings up your proposal as something they might be interested in and they describe the book briefly. *Who's the author?* someone will invariably ask. When your name is mentioned, someone else will say, *That guy? He called me three times yesterday.* Throughout the room, eyes will roll, as if to say, *Who needs it.*

This happens. I've rolled my eyes enough to know what the inside of my skull looks like.

Patience and restraint are valuable traits in authors, and they'll be recognized. And if there's exciting news, it will not take long for it to reach you.

The patient but persistent writer is aware of her target's submission guidelines, which include the requested amount of time to review material. The turnaround time for reading is usually between one and three months, and the wise writer does not contact anyone until that time is up. And when she does, it is with a short, courteous note, call, or e-mail. Not all three. The review period is just an indicator, given as a courtesy, not a contractual obligation. If the agent or house wants to take longer to review material, they can, even though they risk losing the author to a competitor.

If you have given an agent or editor an exclusive look at your work for a specific period of time, do not call until the time period passes. Call or e-mail asking if they'd like a little more time, a week perhaps, to read your submission. You're likely to hear back, but if you do not, send a letter announcing your intent to submit elsewhere but mention that you're still interested in their future consideration. And start all over again.

If they still do not get back to you with any answer, maybe they're the wrong agent or publishing house for you. Just say "Screw 'em," and move on.

We all want to review everything quickly to find the great stuff, but it takes time, sometimes longer than we estimate. Seasonal timing has a lot to do with response times, too. At MacAdam/Cage, April and May are slow months for reading partials, because we're getting ready for BookExpo, the big publishing trade show in early June. After that, however, summer interns show up and there are more hands on deck to read manuscripts and partials. However, New York in August is a publishing ghost town, with everyone working shorter days and weeks so they can go out to the Hamptons. Throughout the year, the priority of submissions fluctuates with other duties. Every literary agency handles submissions differently. There are some times when vetting submissions is a low priority and some times when the mail is eagerly awaited.

Every situation will be slightly different, so good instincts and manners are key. In a way, it's a perverse job interview. You want to project confidence and assert your better qualities without appearing shallow or vain. Agents have their own schedules and do not like to be pushed. Neither do editors, but we're more used to it.

I've had the unpleasant experience of getting irate phone calls from writers demanding to know why it's taken longer than our listing in the *Writer's Market* said it would to review their manuscript. One person was so mad that she filed a complaint with the Better Business Bureau. I had to explain to the BBB that we were not doing business with her and had no legal obligation to her or her submission. Another writer used to leave me angry, drunken phone calls in the middle of the night telling me I was "playing with fire," and he meant it literally because Jesus was the one who told him to write the book.

I can empathize with the frustration of waiting and the emotions it conjures, but they must be held in check. Feeling insulted or ignored is not fun, but again, I promise you the quick answer is not the one you want.

---

9. You Are Flexible

I've heard insanity defined as doing the same thing over and over and expecting a different result each time. I wouldn't call them insane, but there are many writers who submit and submit and submit, always unsuccessfully, never revisiting the quality of their work, analyzing the manner in which they approach the publishing industry, or even tweaking their cover letter. The flexible writer learns from failure.

Sometimes it means rewriting your cover materials or even your book. Sometimes it even means making the painful decision to put a manuscript down and start on a new one. A writer's ability to change direction when his project demands it is a valued skill, and every writer of note has it.

Flexibility in the publishing process means formulating a plan and preparing for contingencies, such as a secondary submission list. It means being prepared for instances in which an agent asks for changes to a manuscript before representing it. In these cases, the writer must decide if the changes will improve the work or if they're a wild goose chase, making the book something it's not supposed to be.

Flexibility may be the deciding factor in getting a book deal. Before making an offer on a book that I think needs work, I'll call the author, with the agent's blessing, just to get a sense of how amenable she might be to making changes. If I sense the author lacks flexibility, I might back off and look for another title. A writer who digs her heels in on every minor change is going to be a difficult edit, and if the book has several problems I do not believe she'll be willing to address, I'll pass.

10. You Learn from Rejection

If you want to be an author, if you want to make a living at it, if writing is how you want to make your mark on the earth—you will begin by being rejected. And the rejection will not be relegated to the professional level; it will be personal as well. You will put your best forth and it will be thrust back at you—most times in patronizing, dismissive, and insulting ways. But if you take every rejection as an indication that you can do better and you act on that, your writing and your publishing career will continue to grow. There's value in rejection. It can steel your resolve to be a better writer and to work harder at getting published, because anger and revenge are powerful motivators. Rejection, when deconstructed to find its genesis, can alert you to missteps you're making. Being passed on, even by a form letter, can help you temper hubris if you let it.

I received my first rejection for a submission to *Boys' Life,* the magazine for Boy Scouts, for a pithy tome on the benefits of using clothes dryer lint to start campfires (it's lightweight and flammable even when wet!). I got a patronizing form letter with a short note mentioning that my idea was not new. They first published this idea long before I was born, and had reiterated the tip a few months before in the magazine. It was even in the official handbook. The tone of the letter led me to believe that the origin of the Scouts themselves may have been due to the excess of lint after the invention of the electric dryer. I may be mistaken, but I recollect the letter ending with the word "Duh!" I was not deflated by this, however, and sent the submission to *The New Yorker,* from which I'm still awaiting Mr. Shawn's reply. Actually, I was so hurt and incensed by the prompt, politely worded slap in the face that I silently attempted to earn a merit badge in cursing out *Boys' Life* under my breath before hanging up my kerchief in disgust and wishing I'd never stolen the whole lint idea from a Weebelo named Dirk.

Of course, I made a mistake. I should have used the

rejection to learn such pearls of wisdom as: "Read the publication you're submitting to," and "Make sure your story idea is fresh." Writing tips for young boys wishing to start big fires was probably a long shot from the beginning.

Rejection is feedback and feedback is valuable. A quick form rejection without comment can alert you that your query or cover letter is in sorry shape. A form rejection with a quick note will tell you that someone found something of some merit in your work to warrant a modicum of respect, that there might be something in it for them in the future if they're not completely dismissive. A long form rejection, with specific notes, is a sure sign of being taken seriously. A call to explain why an agent or editor is passing is an invitation to submit something in the future, perhaps even a rewrite of the same title.

When your work is passed over enough, you may even move from the group of people who say they do not care about rejection slips to the group that does not care about rejection. At the very least, the time spent waiting for an answer back will pass with less anxiety.

---

11. You Take Calculated Risks

I enjoy the unlikely success stories that circulate around publishing, like the writer who forgets his manuscript in the seat pocket of a plane, where it is picked up by a curious flight attendant who gives it to a family member who works in publishing and, voilà, it becomes a bestseller.

My favorite tale is Craig Clevenger's, one of my authors who beat all the odds by doing everything wrong. He sent his first novel, *The Contortionist's Handbook,* around to dozens of agents and publishers and it was rejected with dispatch and little comment. He decided to attend BookExpo America, the largest publishing trade show in the country, thinking an industry Mecca would be prime hunting ground for publishers and agents. What Craig did not know was that the show is rife with fellow rejected-but-not-dejected writers who wander the convention-center floor pushing their manuscripts and singing their own praises. Having no sponsor, writers' badges list only their name and the word *author.* Because the show is mostly for the sales force and the booksellers, unaffiliated authors are spurned and ignored.

Craig's aesthetic style of tattoos and denim is best described as "recently paroled." He spent two days walking the convention floor being shunned. At our booth, he met our art designer, Dorothy Smith, who cared little for what his badge said and was impressed to meet someone not wearing Dockers. After a nice chat, he gave her the only copy of his manuscript that he had brought with him. She not only took it, she read it that night and gave it to me. I could not believe how good the book was. We signed him quickly.

When I tell other editors that we found an author, particularly one as well-thought-of as Craig Clevenger, at the show, they accuse me of lying. A friend who's been in publishing for thirty-five years told me that Craig was the first unagented writer he's ever heard of who got a book deal from attending BEA.

While I love telling the Clevenger saga, I do so here as a cautionary tale. The risk of flying to Chicago to meet

publishers without researching the event or even having a list of publishers he thought would be right for his stuff was pretty dumb, even if it did work out for him. For every exception to the rule, there are a million nonexceptions, wasted attempts where writers put energy and faith—both finite quantities—in long-shot schemes that do not pay off.

But whereas Craig ignored calculated risk in his submission strategy, his writing is the standard for calculated risk. When he set out to write *The Contortionist's Handbook,* he set the bar high. He not only wrote within a genre he read, but he was also determined to add to a body of work he admired in a meaningful way. His calculation was that there was an audience for his story, based on other titles—in his case, the works of Douglas Coupland, Chuck Palahniuk, and Ralph Ellison—but he knew their audiences would be very hostile to an imitator.

He put all his efforts into making the book perfect, no matter how much work it took. He looked at his characters critically to ensure they weren't flat or stereotypical or carbon copies of characters he admired in other authors' books. He sweated over every sentence, every graph, and every chapter. When he finished a draft, he suffered over whether or not every part fit with the whole. He cut finely written pieces that did not fit or were extraneous.

Most important, he was determined from the beginning to be original, to use his own voice and create a cadence and mood previously unwritten. He wanted a plot that hadn't been plowed over by ten thousand titles before his. He wanted to write the first in a new branch of literature, rooted in the body of work he admired but different and all his own. His task entailed incorporating the tenets governing his influences while telling his story in a way no other

story's been told before. I cannot impress enough how difficult this is.

George Carlin wrote, "If people climb Mount Everest
because it's hard, then why do they go up the easy side?"
Craig went up the hard side because no other way would
have satisfied him. If he had watered down his prose or story
to appease conventional publishing wisdom, I doubt he
would have been published, and even if he had been, I do
not think he'd have a career. But he did the work, often at
great personal expense. Now he's as serious as a writer gets.

12. You Take Yourself Seriously

I've made jokes in here at writers' expense and
drawn attention to their flaws and exaggerated them. But I
know how hard it is to write. And I know how hard writers
work.

When I envisioned this book, I wanted to alert writers
to some of the things they're doing wrong that are prevent-
ing them, not from being published, but from even being
taken seriously. I do not know if that wont of mine
stemmed from being a publishing outsider myself or from
some sense of altruism. Agents and editors—myself very
much included—want to find serious writers who care
about their craft and treat their craft as a matter of great import. These are the people who will find respect from readers
and a market over the long haul. The reason we are so skeptical of first-time writers is that they often do not appear to be

serious. I (along with others I know) am of the opinion that these writers just do not yet know what it means to be serious. Ultimately, this whole book is about what it means to be serious. In short, to:

- Do the work so you can feel confident that your book is needed and will be appreciated by a readership.
- Learn how to refine your presentation in order to get the reaction you want.
- Understand the concerns and motivations of the industry you're trying to influence.
- Avoid the sloppy mistakes that make rejecting you easy.
- Separate yourself from those who do not do the necessary work or are looking for shortcuts.
- Keep your wits about you when your efforts aren't working.

If you take yourself seriously and know that your work is valuable and even important, other people will follow suit.

13. You Make Your Own Luck

There's no substitute for luck in publishing. Serendipity just seems to rain her graces down on some and not others. But I would venture that even luck is a byproduct of preparation. You cannot be lucky if you're not ready. If you're trapped in an elevator with überagent Suzanne Gluck for an hour, it's great news for pitching your book. But if your book's not written, or not ready to be read, you're just stuck in an elevator making a fool of yourself. If you submit a query and an editor calls you excitedly to see the manuscript and all you have is the letter, the editor's enthusiasm will likely curdle into disappointment.

Several times I've picked up a manuscript just before the final deadline for a publishing season and found it to be a perfect fit for our list. I've seen books get lucky breaks, like being endorsed by a famous author out of the blue or winning an award we thought was one chance in a million. But every time luck rained down, it was because the book was deserving.

Luck's nice, but it's not really a mandatory ingredient in success. What's really lucky is really enjoying the act of writing.

14. You Have Fun

When an author has joy about creating his work, it comes through in his writing, even if it's a business book or some other form of simply imparting straightforward information. We digest information more pleasantly if the writer seems excited to tell us what he knows.

In fiction, a writer's sense of pleasure affects every plot thread and character trait. It also influences little things like the turn of a phrase or a nuanced moment. I've read a lot of manuscripts and often get into a writer's groove and get a sense of what's coming next. Every now and again when I'm reading, I'll notice how a writer spent the time to avoid a cliché or put extra effort into making a utilitarian sentence more exciting. And I'll know that this writer loves language and has strived to keep it engaging and fresh.

Writing is hard and feels like pulling out your own teeth at times, and the humbling, and often humiliating, act of trying to get published can shred your self-confidence. To paraphrase a famous politician's line about the Irish, what's the point of being a writer if the world doesn't break your heart once in a while? With all the anguish and bother, it's still worth it. The grief, pain, and sorrow writers experience are easily bested by the delight of looking at the page and realizing that they've exceeded their highest expectations and satisfied even their own worst doubts.

I've had the pure pleasure of calling many writers and telling them that MacAdam/Cage would like to publish their book, a good few times completely out of the blue. I like to think I'm a tough nut to crack, but making that call always gets me. It is the best part of my job. I'm always a little envious when the agent gets the privilege.

No matter how much trouble the writer's gone to, or how many sacrifices she's made, none of them I know would ever say it wasn't worth it. Because it is.

FOR THE BEST IN PAPERBACKS, LOOK FOR THE

In every corner of the world, on every subject under the sun, Penguin represents quality and variety—the very best in publishing today.

For complete information about books available from Penguin—including Penguin Classics, Penguin Compass, and Puffins—and how to order them, write to us at the appropriate address below. Please note that for copyright reasons the selection of books varies from country to country.

In the United States: Please write to *Penguin Group (USA), P.O. Box 12289 Dept. B, Newark, New Jersey 07101-5289* or call 1-800-788-6262.

In the United Kingdom: Please write to *Dept. EP, Penguin Books Ltd, Bath Road, Harmondsworth, West Drayton, Middlesex UB7 0DA*.

In Canada: Please write to *Penguin Books Canada Ltd, 10 Alcorn Avenue, Suite 300, Toronto, Ontario M4V 3B2*.

In Australia: Please write to *Penguin Books Australia Ltd, P.O. Box 257, Ringwood, Victoria 3134*.

In New Zealand: Please write to *Penguin Books (NZ) Ltd, Private Bag 102902, North Shore Mail Centre, Auckland 10*.

In India: Please write to *Penguin Books India Pvt Ltd, 11 Panchsheel Shopping Centre, Panchsheel Park, New Delhi 110 017*.

In the Netherlands: Please write to *Penguin Books Netherlands bv, Postbus 3507, NL-1001 AH Amsterdam*.

In Germany: Please write to *Penguin Books Deutschland GmbH, Metzlerstrasse 26, 60594 Frankfurt am Main*.

In Spain: Please write to *Penguin Books S. A., Bravo Murillo 19, 1° B, 28015 Madrid*.

In Italy: Please write to *Penguin Italia s.r.l., Via Benedetto Croce 2, 20094 Corsico, Milano*.

In France: Please write to *Penguin France, Le Carré Wilson, 62 rue Benjamin Baillaud, 31500 Toulouse*.

In Japan: Please write to *Penguin Books Japan Ltd, Kaneko Building, 2-3-25 Koraku, Bunkyo-Ku, Tokyo 112*.

In South Africa: Please write to *Penguin Books South Africa (Pty) Ltd, Private Bag X14, Parkview, 2122 Johannesburg*.